Monica,

Tial of Support

97

RENEWING APOSTOLIC RELIGIOUS LIFE

Renewing Apostolic
Religious Life

by

David Coghlan SJ

the columba press

First published in 1997 by
the columba press
55A Spruce Avenue, Stillorgan Industrial Park,
Blackrock, Co Dublin

Cover by Bill Bolger
Origination by The Columba Press
Printed in Ireland by Colour Books Ltd, Dublin

ISBN 1 85607 177 4

Copyright © 1996, David Coghlan SJ

Contents

Introduction   7

PART 1: THE ORGANISATIONAL DYNAMICS OF RELIGIOUS LIFE   11

Chapter 1   Levels of Participation in Apostolic Religious Life   15

Chapter 2   Planning for Strategic Action   26

Chapter 3   Strategic Leadership   39

PART 2: MANAGING CHANGE AND RENEWAL   55

Chapter 4   Understanding Change   59

Chapter 5   Managing Apostolic Change   71

Chapter 6   Phases and Levels of Apostolic Renewal   84

Chapter 7   Groups in the Renewal Process   94

Chapter 8   Provincial Assemblies   110

Chapter 9   Consultation and Facilitation   121

Chapter 10   The Art of Leading Apostolic Renewal   131

References and Further Reading   136

Introduction

This is an 'organisational' book, that is, it focuses on religious orders as organisations. Its purpose is to unravel something of the complexity of the inner and outer life of religious orders. The inner life comprises the rich spirituality and charism of the order – its desires to serve God's people out of a particular tradition in the church. The outer life flows from the inner life and is what members of religious orders actually do – teach in schools, work in hospitals, run social agencies, work with the deprived, direct people in prayer and so on. This outer life has two dimensions – the purposeful planning and choice of ministries which characterise what the order judges to be important in the light of charism and the daily task of doing it. This inner and outer life are the bedrock of religious apostolic ministry and are the source of energy. Harmonising them is the key to facilitating that energy. The fact that this book focuses primarily on the outer dimension is not to minimise the importance of the mystery of the inner.

This book focuses on the organisational dynamics of religious ministry. Accordingly, it addresses particular features of organisational life, especially with regard to managing renewal and change. When a large group of people, spread over a geographical region or across the world, attempts to renew its articulation of its purposes, its priorities and make changes in the light of such a renewal, then a great deal of organisational processes come into play.

Religious life and ministry is clearly undergoing massive transformation. Not only have the old artifacts (large numbers, big houses, complete ownership and control of institutions) gone, but the core assumptions of what it is to be a religious is changing also.

Organisation development, or OD as it is generally called, is an applied behavioural science approach to understanding and managing change in organisations. By applied behavioural science is meant the application of individual and group psychology, organisational theory, sociology, anthropology and so on to understanding how change takes place in human systems. Organisation development differs from other approaches to change in that it emphasises the facilitative approach, whereby members of an organisation are helped to manage their own change.

Can behavioural science be applied to religious ministry? When we view the complexity of processes such as articulating vision, values and priorities, taking concerted action, developing leadership, forming ministry teams and so on, the answer is clearly Yes. As, for example, spiritual direction has benefitted from and built on the theory and practice of counselling and psychotherapy, so the renewal of religious ministries can benefit from the learning which has been accumulated from the organisational sciences.

To whom is this book addressed? There are four audiences. First, major superiors (generals, provincials, regional superiors) and directors of apostolates will find it useful in exercising their roles within their orders or ministries. Second, the many people, religious and lay, who work as consultants and facilitators with religious organisations, will use it as a resource for their own work. Thirdly, religious who are not in executive roles within their apostolates will find it helps them participate in their teams and assist their understanding of the change issues facing their ministries. Finally, the secular OD readership will find the application of the theory and practice of OD to religious organisations interesting.

On a practical note, I have struggled with language and terminology in this book. As this book is aimed at both major superiors (generals, provincials and regional superiors) and directors of apostolates, rather than complicating terms, I have used 'provincial' throughout the text to be inclusive of a wide range of organisational leaders. Similarly, to avoid the complexities of terms like 'religious order', 'religious congregation', I have used 'province' to be descriptive of a juridical region with multiple apostolates, which could also refer to a world-wide order. In an attempt to resolve the perennial issue of inclusive and exclusive pronouns, I have used the plural, 'they', and 'their' where appropriate.

Acknowledgements

While the visible outcome of a work project such as a book is a text which appears under my name alone, the process to that outcome is a co-operative venture. There are many who have helped in diverse ways whom I wish to acknowledge and without whom I would not have completed or even begun.

Many of the chapters are developments of previously published articles. *Human Development* published earlier versions of: chapter 1 (Winter 1988); chapter 2, (Summer 1987); chapter 5, (Summer 1990); chapter 6, (Fall 1991) and chapter 7, (Winter 1994). My thanks to James Gill SJ and Linda Amadeo for their continual support over many years and permission to use this material. *Review for Religious* published earlier versions of chapter 2 (July-August 1989) and chapter 8 (November-December 1994). I thank David Fleming SJ for permission to use this material. *Religious Life Review* published earlier versions of chapter 7 (November-December 1990) and chapter 9 (September-October 1987). My thanks to Austin Flannery OP. My gratitude goes to Rachel McKee of Scientific Methods, Austin, Texas who read a draft of chapter 4 and provided valuable guidance on the Grid® material and also facilitated granting permission for its reproduction.

My deepest gratitude is owed to Joe Dargan SJ, Cara Nagle RCE and Colette Stevenson PBVM who took time to make valuable comments on a draft and shared their experience and insights to strengthen the text. Alan Fitzpatrick skillfully took my handwritten diagrams and translated them into graphics.

There are those from whom I have learned the theory and practice of organisation development, particularly my mentor and friend Ed Schein, Dick Ottaway and Jesuit brothers, Philip Harnett SJ and Nicholas Rashford SJ. There is an extensive and anonymous group of clients – provincials and councils of different religious orders, who over the years have engaged me to work with them and have taught me much about the process of apostolic renewal. This book is the fruit of their work and, in some respects, they are the true authors. Finally, and not least, I thank the members of my community, Pat and David, for their love and encouragement.

David Coghlan
October 1996

PART 1

The Organisational Dynamics of Religious Life

In taking an organisation development approach to religious life and ministry it is useful to look first at the properties of organisations. A standard definition defines an organisation as, 'the planned co-ordination of the activities of a number of people for the achievement of some common explicit purpose or goal, through the division of labour and function, and through a hierarchy of authority and responsibility'.

Organisations are fundamentally about co-ordinating effort. For a small group, co-ordination may be relatively simple, but as group size increases co-ordination becomes more complex. When there are hundreds or thousands of members, spread across the world or a specific geographical region, formal co-ordination mechanisms become critical. For co-ordination to be successful there needs to be common purposes and aims and agreement about what is to be achieved. The third property of organisations is the division of labour and function, that is, the different tasks to be done to achieve common purposes are distinguished, hopefully on the basis of what is needed and individuals' talents and gifts to do them. Finally, these activities need to be integrated, hence the need for super-ordinate groups or individuals to have primary responsibility for leading and managing these activities.

It must be noted that the term 'organisation' is not synonymous with the term 'business'. Some religious tend to confuse these terms and so get irate to think that business principles are being applied to religious life. The term 'organisation' applies to the co-ordination of effort, as I have described, and so applies to very many contexts. Indeed, ironically, the language of organisations has taken in some religious terms, mission being the most obvious one. There is cur-

rently a movement to understand the role of spirituality in organisations.

The religious order or the province of a religious order or the apostolate of a religious order is an organisation. There are common
aims and purposes arising from the call of the gospel and the vision
of the founder, as expressed in constitutions and contemporary
chapter documents. There is need for co-ordination of activities –
some religious are teaching, others work in drop-in centres, some
are directing others in prayer, and all these activities are spread
across a geographical region. There is need for integration so there
are leadership structures whose responsibilities are defined as leading these multiple activities.

There are many different shapes which organisations take. The one
we tend to be most familiar with is the formal hierarchical model,
based on the military or bureaucratic model, with clear vertical
lines of authority and responsibility. This model predominated in
religious life up to relatively recently and is now being replaced in
many orders by a more organic model, where leadership is being
understood in more collegial terms. This book doesn't presume any
particular organisational form, and while terms like *provincial* are
used, this is more out of convenience than advocating a particular
organisational model.

Organisations are not simply about the formalisation of the proper-
ties discussed above. They lead two lives – the formal life presented
in terms of the documentation describing purpose, values, goals,
activities, resources, assets and so on, and the informal life of experience, norms, culture, traditions. These two lives are typically
depicted in terms of an iceberg.

The formal life of a religious order is found in its constitutions,
chapter documents, statements of charism, plans, structures, number of apostolates, ages of members, resources, financial and material assets and so on. This is information which can be gathered by
examining documentation and looking at the communities and
apostolates from the outside. This part of an organisation's life is
formal and didactic, and is represented as the part of the iceberg
showing above the water line.

The other life is hidden, informal and experiential. This represents

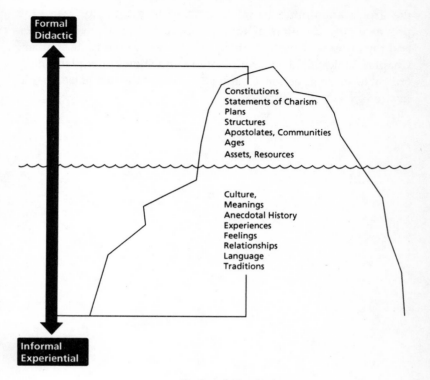

The Organisational Iceberg

the lived experience of the members, what one only learns by being part of it – the cultural assumptions and the norms surrounding traditions, the meanings members attribute to ways of doing things, the particular language used within the order, peoples' experiences and feelings, the anecdotal history of the order or province or particular communities, memories of formation, how people remember the changes since Vatican II – these are all elements of organisational life that are hidden below the water line. As with icebergs, what is below the water and out of sight is larger than what is visible above the water line and is very powerful.

Structure of Part 1

Part 1 has three chapters. Chapter 1 describes how a religious order comprises four inter-related and inter-dependent levels of participation – the individual who is serving God out of a personal call, the group attempting to work together in a ministry team, the province co-ordination of multiple ministries and communities, and the order serving the church and the world out of its charism. Chapter 2 takes strategy and planning and shows how planning is critical to strategic action. Chapter 3 examines the role of leadership in strategy.

CHAPTER 1

Levels of Participation
in Apostolic Religious Life

There are four levels of participation in apostolic religious life (Figure 1-1). They are as follows: an individual level, or level one, is the action of the individual in a contract to belong and be part of the religious order. The second level, or level two, is the interaction of the individual working in a face-to-face team in ministry. The third level is the interaction of a province (region) as an aggregate of many ministry teams to produce effective ministry. The fourth level is the order's action as a single actor in an external environment, responding to needs and issues in apostolic endeavours according to its charism.

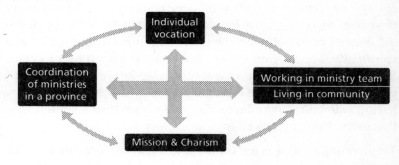

Figure 1-1
Levels of Participation in Apostolic
Religious Life

As perspective broadens there are other levels; a fifth level which is defined by general membership of the church, a sixth which would encompass inter-church and inter-faith relations and so on. This model is not absolute as many aspects overlap from one level to another or from one point of view to another. They are delineated here to help understand behaviour in a religious life context, enabling religious and religious superiors to be better able to utilise the apostolic resources in a co-ordinated manner.

LEVEL I: INDIVIDUAL

The basic unit of a religious order is the individual. The individual joins the order out of a sense of a call from God which is individual and personal to that individual and which finds expression in membership of that particular order. Individuals typically begin through a temporary probationary relationship with the order, through candidature, postulancy and novitiate (according to the norms of that order). During the period of probation individuals get to know the order while the order, through its formation procedures, tests the individual's candidacy for membership. When this period of formation is completed to the order's satisfaction, the individual is admitted to membership of the order, through temporary profession, and enters a further programme of formation – studies, training, ministry and community living.

From the point of view of the individual and the order's superiors, the process is one of bonding. The individual, in following a sense of God's call, enters into a tentative relationship with the order and then, over a period, grows into bonding within the order, i.e. defining himself or herself with the order and internalising the order's spirituality, norms, culture and traditions. The bonding process is formalised through the profession of religious vows. The order's superiors also engage in a bonding process with the individual – by testing suitability and adaptability and committing themselves to that individual's membership.

The bonding process is not confined to the initial formation period. Individual religious grow in their understanding of this process as they move through their life cycle and reflect on their experiences in ministry, community life, retreats and other experiences. Individuals' growth and development with regard to their relationship with the order and their work in ministry are facilitated by their engagement in spiritual direction. Through spiritual direction individual religious can attend to the issues which emerge in their life and explore them in a context of prayer and development. The superiors' perspective on this process is that the individual religious belong to the order through an appropriate psychological and religious contract and so they respond to individuals by forming a context and environment attractive to the development of the individual vocation. This is formalised, not only through initial formation, but also through the ongoing relationship between the individual and the provincial superior, as well as through particular structured events individuals may utilise from time to time, such as special courses, sabbaticals and meetings related to the ongoing life of the order.

The bonding relationship between an individual religious and the order does not develop in one direction automatically. Individuals may become disaffected with their life in the order. They may, through particular experiences in ministry or community or in the face of superiors' decisions which they could not accept, become alienated from their superiors and their peers and settle for a life of disaffection. There are those who become afflicted by addictions or illness, whether physical or mental. There are those who come to the conclusion that the focus of their life lies elsewhere and who leave the order. An order's membership typically comprises those who are active and committed, those who are alienated and disaffected, those who are ill and those who are elderly and retired. All are equally members of the order and live in a bonded relationship with the order.

The Individual Level is one of four levels.

The Level I relationship between the individual and the order is the bedrock of religious life and so it must be managed. Such a management involves different approaches to meet the issues of the different bonding relationships which exist. For some, the forms of community in which they live, the ministry they exercise, continuing formation activities, participation in assemblies, chapters and so on, nurture their life in the order. For others, being cared for and being supported in their life restricted by ill-health or old age, are what is appropriate. Others need special help of a therapeutic nature. At the same time, it must be recognised that the individual level is one of four levels and that the management of any one level is integrally linked to each of the others.

LEVEL II: FACE-TO-FACE MINISTRY TEAM

A second more complex level exists when the individual participates in ministry teams and in community. Level II describes this apostolic and team level. Having a sense of belonging (Level I), the individual now contributes to collective ventures by forming team with ministry colleagues, and probably living in community. From the individual's point of view, entry into ministry and community involves interfacing with other individuals (including lay colleagues) in clearly defined units, which I am calling face-to-face ministry teams. Teams are typically defined in terms of: (i) face-to-face interaction, (ii) common goals, (iii) psychological awareness of other members, and (iv) self-definition as a team with member-nonmember boundaries defined to some degree.

Effectiveness on this level means that a team is effective in its ministry and in the internal working relationships among its members. The individual team member's task within the face-to-face ministry team is to contribute to the team's functioning, while the team's task is to be a functioning unit. The superiors' perspective is that the team be significant in its work in terms of the overall apostolic endeavour. Accordingly, it is the function of superiors and directors of apostolates to facilitate the team in its awareness, reflection and learning on the team level.

Team building is the process whereby team members learn the skills of working together.

Team-building is the process whereby team members learn the skills of working together and of managing their own collective reflection whereby they can learn from their shared experiences. Team-building focuses on the team's activities in: (i) setting goals and priorities, (ii) analysing and allocating work, (iii) examining the team's process, and (iv) examining the interpersonal relationships between team members and between the individual and the team. Within the team there are different roles and perspectives on each of these activities. Other significant interventions focus on less comprehensive issues and provide significant skills to the team. Typically these are general process consultation skills in functional behaviour, communication, problem-solving, decision-making, leadership and norm evaluation. Team development provides a framework for understanding the growth stages of the collective personality that is the team, and through cultural analysis uncovering the hidden assumptions that constitute its relationship to the internal and external environment.

Another application of this second level can be found in the dynamics of community living. When religious live in community and attempt to share life in terms of core issues of faith and charism, apostolic ministry and domestic arrangements, the dynamics of groups, albeit different from those of ministry groups, are present. A community develops its own norms of communication and decision-making which aim at supporting the individual's religious and apostolic life. Critical issues focus on the quality of life, the fit between domestic arrangements and apostolic activity, and the community's openness to noncommunity members. Decisions around the sharing of faith, community prayer and availability of the members to each other tend to be central to the resolution of these critical issues.

The spirituality of this second level is built around the shared sense of charism and how it is experienced by the individual members. For a collective spirituality to develop, the members of a group must engage in sharing what the charism means to them individually, how it impacts on their lives as they are lived, and for a mutual influencing to exist among the group.

LEVEL III: PROVINCE

From the team's point of view, to be effective and to enter into the life of the order is to work within a larger system. The province level is Level III. This level is made up of multiple face-to-face ministry teams and communities in a jurisdiction which must function together to accomplish province goals. The province level must have the ability to pass beyond the boundaries of individual ministries in order to implement programmes that involve multiple ministries, especially different ones. The team's task within the province is to perform as a team while having a sense of belonging to the province from whose provincial it receives its mission and scarce resource. The processes of integrating the work of teams around a common vision and of distributing scarce resources, such as personnel and money, are the key activities of the province level. So in a province this means an effective blending of such apostolates as education, pastoral, spiritual etc. in a planned co-ordinated manner which reflects province priorities. The province must be capable of finding its own dysfunction. A correction process includes the integrating of competing or independently oriented apostolic units into a unified functioning unit that is the province level. There can be difficulties when the skills for reflective and corrective action on this province level are not present. Individual ministries feel no responsibility for other ministries, are antagonistic towards provincials when they want to move an individual from one ministry to another, and pressurise them for resources for 'their' apostolate. Provincials have a difficult task in enabling the members of a province to think 'province' and act on this level. Province assemblies are frequently used as a means for developing and sustaining awareness and ownership of a sense of province.

Strategic management, whereby the expressed, chosen, strategic direction of the province's apostolic thrust is co-ordinated among the interrelated systems of the province, is the mechanism for achieving effectiveness on this third level. Typically it involves setting priorities or having a view of the many ministries of the province which helps articulate how they stand in relation to each other in terms of future development, closure or hand over. It includes a plan of how religious personnel might be deployed and how collaborative structures with non-religious colleagues might be evolved.

This means that in order that the selected significant plans be implemented they must be supported by systems of good communication, regular review and appropriate structure. The motivation to identify with and work for the strategy must be facilitated. Province plans need to be integrated into province structures, such as province assemblies and chapters and inter-community events. So the Level III tasks are implemented through multiple interventions – structural, educational, formative – so that the interdependence of the systems within the province work well together and complement each other.

Another key mechanism for integrating ministries at Level III is the use of provincial commissions or task forces. Many provinces have standing commissions with briefs on such areas of ministry as secondary education, formation, pastoral ministry. These commissions perform different functions. They may act as advisors to the provincial or co-ordinators of policy. What may be neglected is the role commissions can play in helping build ownership of provincial policy in a province.

An example of Level III can be seen in a region of one particular order which, in formulating plans, realised that it did not have the structures to facilitate implementation of what it wanted to do. Accordingly, the province was divided into 'sectors', that is general groupings based on particular apostolic activities in the province's ministries. These included, among others, education, pastoral, social, and formation. They corresponded to the actual apostolates administered by the province – schools, parishes, etc. Each sector was assigned a 'delegate'. This was not a juridical office but more a role whereby sectors could reflect on their ministry. The delegate had the task of co-ordinating planning and review in his own part-icular sector and working with the provincial and provincial staff on a ministries commission that reflected on the province as a whole and integrated the processes of each sector. Through this newly constituted structure, a common approach on an area of min-istry could be co-ordinated. This co-ordination is from a province perspective. From the perspective of the individual ministries with-in a sector, teams, which hitherto did not have an easy facility for relating to other teams in the same ministry, could now be linked through a process that emphasised their common experiences, the direction in which they were going, and their communion within the province. The competition for and allocation of the scarce resources of religious personnel could be managed.

This third level reflects the complexity of multiple ministries which require co-ordination in a jurisdict-ion. It is the third stage of complexity after the individual and the team. It is not limited to any particular form of structure which an order might adopt. While terms like 'province' and 'provincial' are being used in this book, this third level is not exclusive of newer organic models of structure which exist in many orders.

> *This third level reflects the complexity of multiple ministries which require co-ordination in a jurisdiction.*

LEVEL IV: CHARISM AND MISSION

The order's task is to minister to the contemporary world according to the spirit of its constitutions. The charism and mission level of an order requires the ability of the order to map its internal resources as well as mapping the external environment. The basic goal of

Level IV is to participate in such a way that the order works as a unit in its external world in the process of evangelisation. The ingredients at this level consist in a deep-rooted united spirituality of the order's charism and its mission in the church, an assessment of the internal resources of the order, a knowledge of the external world, integrated to form an articulated direction for that order in the concrete world in a given time frame. The difficulties lie in the area of an inability to respond to change, either in terms of the changing contemporary world or of internal culture.

The order's task is to minister to the contemporary world according to the spirit of its constitutions.

The key intervention at this level is the 'strategic planning' framework in which the anchor is the charism of the order. It is out of a clear and united sense of identity that internal resources can be combined with external analysis to provide the framework for prayerfully discerning significant direction for an order's apostolic ventures. External analysis can be done through social analysis and open systems planning, both of which are tools for critically evaluating significant environmental forces relevant to apostolic activity. Typically, the integration of charism with apostolic choice is done through the selection of criteria and discernment of options. These criteria emerge from the order's foundation experiences and are given a contemporary articulation. The process of attracting new members occurs on this level.

INTER-LEVEL DYNAMICS

The four levels within a religious order are distinct and separate, which means that particular interventions can only be effective if they are addressing the correct issues. Level II dynamics are different from those at Level I. If a team's inability to manage change is due to its difficulties in establishing or meeting goals, getting the work done, ineffective or inappropriate communication or decision-making processes, then Level II team-building interventions are pertinent. If the issues in the team boil down to particular individuals' personal issues with regard to themselves and their relationship to the order, then Level I interventions, such as counselling, are appropriate.

Level I and II issues are brought to the Level III situation. A ministry team's self-perception can affect its relationship to other ministry teams. The creation of a sense of province is difficult because individuals and teams typically view the province from the limited perspective of their own ministry or community. Development of a sense of province frequently only comes from holding an office that provokes one to think province (provincial) or participation in provincial chapters or assemblies. Province assemblies have become more widely used as mechanisms for generating an awareness of province. Developing a Level III awareness and ownership is a slow process. Again, what is essential is that Level III issues and dynamics be distinguished from those of Levels I and II.

All the levels are integrally linked to one another. Each level affects and is affected by each of the others. An example of their inter-dependence and inter-relatedness can be seen in the Jesuits' experience of the development of the spirit- *Each level affects and is* uality of justice and its centrality for *affected by each of the others.* Jesuit life and ministry. The reformulation of the Society's mission in terms of 'the service of faith of which the promotion of justice is an absolute requirement' (a Level IV activity) came through the work of the church in Latin America and articulated in the Synod of Bishops in 1971 (Level V). This decree of the 32nd General Congregation, 'Our Mission Today', made organisational demands on each province of the Society. Provinces had to review their ministries in the light of this reformulation (Level III). Individual apostolic teams, in turn, took 'Our Mission Today' and applied it to their own ministry (Level II). The decree demanded a change in the individual Jesuit's sense of identity resulting in many Jesuits feeling re-energised in their relationship to the Society and others, unable to identify with the new direction, felt marginalised and that it was no longer the order they joined (Level I). In this example, the movement is from Level V through IV to III to II to I.

What happens in a ministry team or community affects how individuals can feel about their life and work. If individuals are having personal problems or are disaffected by their life, they can behave in a dysfunctional manner and disrupt the work of a team or life in community. Decisions at provincial level regarding allocation of personnel affect the work of ministry teams and the life of communities and so on.

Discernment is the critical element of inter-level dynamics in the apostolic religious life. Individual religious are expected to engage in discernment, not only in terms of their own life and mission (Level I), but also in having the dispositions to participate in communal and apostolic discernment in common (Level II). While it is considerably more difficult to organise and manage logistically, a province must be able to engage in apostolic discernment (Level III). For a province to discern, its individual members and apostolic teams and communities must have the dispositions and skills of discernment.

The levels are central to the process of change in any organisation. For change to take root in a large complex system like a religious order or a province, key individuals have to recognise the need for change, and change. Apostolic teams and communities have to apply themselves to the change agenda. The change must be generalised across the province. Individuals may have to change what they do or how they do it. The change process involves reactions to the change issues by individuals, teams and communities in order to move from a stage of disconfirmation to a renewed ministry. The continuous rounds of meetings, consultations and discernments, which characterise the dynamics of change, illustrate how the change agenda progresses through an organisation as individuals and teams/communities deal with the change issues and move the change to the wider system across the province. This will be dealt with in more detail in Chapter 6.

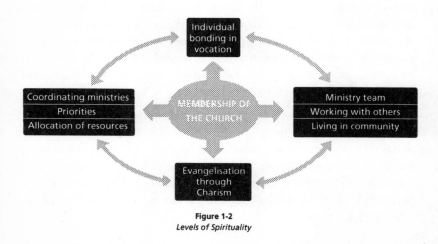

Figure 1-2
Levels of Spirituality

Levels are key to understanding corporate spirituality. The individual's spirituality grows through prayer and life in the order. That is strengthened and reinforced by living in community and working in ministry teams and further reinforced by participation in a wider system of other ministries. These three levels reinforce and give concrete life to the spirituality of the order (Figure 1-2).

CONCLUSIONS

There is an extensive literature on apostolic religious life – on the prayer of religious, on religious formation, apostolic renewal and community life. This literature is aimed at helping religious understand the dynamics of religious life and develop so as to participate more effectively in ministry. Because of the complexity of the task and the volume of the literature, the process of how religious function in their orders may not be well articulated. The relationship between an individual's inner motivations and apostolic life, how that apostolic life is lived out in ministry with others in a complex interrelationship with other ministries in a changing world and limited resources, is typically hard to grasp. The four levels of participation in apostolic religious life described are an attempt to unravel this complexity (Figure 1-1). If a provincial is sensitive to these four levels of operation and can understand how to intervene appropriately in such a way that individuals, teams, provinces, and the order itself can come to understand its own behaviour, then effective change can take place. The formation teacher can utilise this framework to give religious in formation a model from which they can participate more fully in the life of the order. The spiritual director can use it in mapping different issues that emerge in spiritual direction contexts. For the consultant, it provides a significant diagnostic tool in working with religious orders on renewal processes.

CHAPTER 2

Planning for Strategic Action

Many religious orders have used and are using the notion of strategy and its application in strategic planning and management in the renewal of their ministries. Strategy is an organisational process whereby the impact of a changing world is juxtaposed with the resources of the religious order and significant decisions are made in the light of the order's mission and charism. An essential issue is that religious engage in strategic processes in a manner that is consonant with the type of organisations religious orders are and with the religious faith which is attentive to the voice of the Holy Spirit.

> Strategy for the religious order is the pattern of decisions in the order that determines and reveals its charism, purposes or goals, produces the principal policies and plans for achieving those goals, and defines the kind of community it is or intends to be, and the nature of its apostolic activities in relation to different constituencies.

Strategy for a school, hospital or any apostolic ministry is defined in similar terms. What is essential with regard to strategy that it is fundamentally a qualitative mode of thinking. Strategy is most easily contrasted with the notion of *operational*. Operational refers to the activities that maintain the running of the operation. Superiors can often be in need of help in making the distinction between strategic and operational. An apostolate may be very well run and maintained in good order (operational planning and management) and lacking in broad vision of where it is developing in the future in the light of its vision and the changing world (strategic planning and management). It would be a mistake to equate strategic and long-term planning. Strategic is of a different quality from long-term. An apostolate can have a long-term plan regarding a new building without ever thinking of it in strategic terms. The creation of a province plan can be viewed operationally (We need a plan to map out the tasks to be done over the next few years) or strategically (How do we move into the future in a way that enables us to minister from our charism in the light of changing times, new demands and reduced personnel?).

Henry Mintzberg, a leading writer on strategy, explores the concept in terms of five 'Ps': plan, ploy, pattern, position and perspective (Figure 2-1). Strategy as *plan* refers to consciously intended courses of action, whether general or specific, which are made in advance of actions to which they apply. Strategy as *ploy* is part of strategy as plan and refers to a manner in which an organisation may hope to gain an advantage in a situation to achieve its ends. Strategy as *pattern* is about consistency of behaviour, in that strategy may be inferred from what is decided and what happens. In this way, having no strategy may indeed be a strategy! Strategy as *position* refers to where an organisation locates itself in its external environment and what its values are. Strategy as *perspective* focuses the importance of a world view – that strategy represents a shared, collective way of perceiving the world.

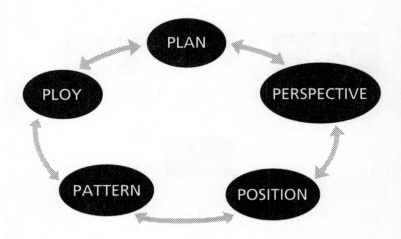

Figure 2-1
Mintzberg's 5 Ps

Each of the five 'Ps' applies to strategy as it is practised by religious orders. Many orders have produced a plan and have included ploys in it, for example to get government funding. How an order is managing change and preparing for the future reveals its strategic pattern whether intended or not. Very many orders use strategy as position as they attempt to implement an option for the poor. Strategy is a perspective on the world in that it represents a view that change is constant and that an apostolic order is continually seeking for how its charism and mission might be fulfilled in a changing world.

THE ELEMENTS OF STRATEGY

There are four elements in strategy: core mission, environmental scan, internal review and strategic posture (Figure 2-2). Each of these elements contributes an essential ingredient to the strategy process.

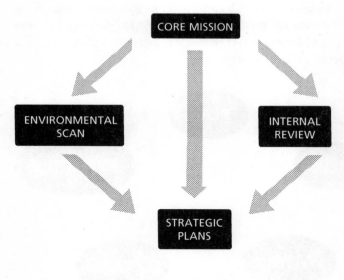

Figure 2-2
Elements of Strategy

The core mission (charism) is the order's constitutions and the reflection on the life of the founder and the order's early history as articulated for the contemporary world. The charism provides the fundamental identity of the order. Core mission is the expression of the order's basic charism as articulated in constitutions, chapter decrees, the life and writings of the founder and the early history. The mandate from Vatican II for religious orders to return to their original inspiration launched a rediscovery of the founders' inspiration and a re-articulation of that inspiration in contemporary terms. The purpose of studying the life, words and works of the founder is to articulate in the contemporary world the founder's authentic vision so that it can become an ideal and norm for contemporary renewal and adaptation. Similarly, the early history of the order provides a model of how the founder's vision was put into practice and gives life and meaning to the written abstraction which is the constitutions, which were typically written down after a period of apostolic experience. The cultural assumptions beneath the stated and actual behaviour are uncovered in the history of the order. This process provides a framework for understanding a model for the contemporary reformulation of the order's core mission. Knowing the core mission, or having a sense of identity, is but one element in the picture. Of itself it does not lead to clarity of action.

Environmental scanning is the process of reading the signs of the times and interpreting them in the light of the gospel. It is the process of social analysis and theological reflection. It goes beyond the merely descriptive and attempts to formulate causal factors in social situations and therefore provides the basis for which apostolic choices can be made. Mapping the environment involves naming those who have a 'stake' in the outcome of the order's ministries, identifying what demands these stakeholders are making, seeing how the order is currently responding and projecting future demands.

All this is integrally linked to charism. The results of the environmental scanning are examined in the context of the order's mission and integrated into the arena in which the order ministers and wishes to minister. It provides the framework for clarifying the complexity of the outside world with which the religious apostolate is confronted, and provides the unifying framework for the planning process. Yet core mission and environmental scanning are insufficient for planning. Unless the planning is grounded in the actual resources of the order, it is unreal.

The internal review maps the resources of the order in qualitative and quantitative terms. The qualitative terms review the quality of apostolic activities, while the quantitative reviews actual and potential resources – personnel, skills, property, finances, etc. In the quantitative dimension, religious orders' resources have shifted considerably in recent years. The inverted pyramid of the age structure of most religious orders has led to the divestiture of large proper-ties, the formalisation of ownership of apostolic institutions in trusts and corporations, and shared ministry with lay colleagues. In the qualitative dimension, reviewing the quality of apostolic activities and assessing strengths and weaknesses complement core mission and the environmental scan.

> *The process of moving from charism to strategic plan requires appropriate uses of rational analysis, judgement and prayeful discernment.*

In many respects there has been a significant shift in the formulation of the internal review. Formerly, the review would have had a focus on the religious order very much – its numbers, ages, finances, etc. Now, given the numbers and ages of actual religious and the devolved nature of ownership and administrative structures of many apostolates, the internal review includes the quality of relationship with lay colleagues and the nature of flexibility in contracted relationships, and so the review takes in a wider constituency.

These three elements of core mission, environmental scan and internal review, are integrated to form the basis of the strategic posture, which comprises the primary issues to be addressed in a concrete time period, typically the next three to five years (Figure 2-3). This is the actual strategic planning stage in which goals are set. The goals are the result of all the preceding analysis and should be expressed in such a way so as to convey a sense of the critical tasks that must be dealt with over the given time frame, and the financial costs associated with such tasks. The process of moving from charism to strategic posture through environmental scanning and internal review is a process that requires appropriate uses of rational analysis, judgement and prayerful discernment. The four steps are integrally linked. A sense of charism is needed to ground any planning. A sense of charism needs the outward-looking thrust based on experience of the contemporary world. Planning needs to be realistic in terms of the actual resources of the order, including financial.

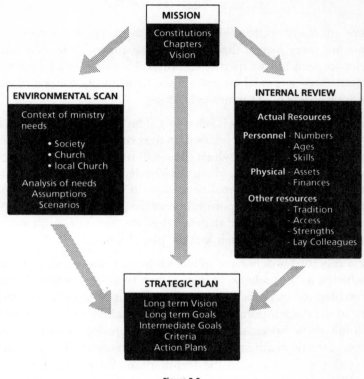

Figure 2-3
Strategic planning

Strategic planning and action are integrally linked to the five levels. Strategy itself takes place on Level IV and V – that is in terms of the order's mission in the church. Then, strategic decisions have to be implemented at Level III across the province – resulting in, for example, a re-ordering of priorities, a movement of personnel or resources or opening a new apostolate. Implementation takes place at a local level in an apostolate and community (Level II) and may involve individuals receiving a new mission or adapting their way of working (Level I). A provincial, superior and director of work each has his or her own part in this complex movement across the levels. For instance, the director of work has a responsibility for implementing the change at local level and building the team around the new focus of ministry. This may also involve helping individual team members adapt, a role which may also involve the local superior.

APPROACHES TO STRATEGY

There are many approaches to how a strategic plan is formulated. Some are more formal than others; some appear to be disjointed. Any approach has its own strengths and weaknesses. I shall now present three approaches and review them in the context of how religious orders plan for strategic action.

One approach to strategy is what might be termed the 'grand plan' approach. This approach is based on the premise that a comprehensive plan be formulated, which covers all the key aspects. It articulates central assumptions, identifies key decisions and names what is to be done. It is a formal process with procedures of analysis, planning and action. Responsibility for the process lies in the hands of the provincial as *the* strategist. When the plan is articulated it is implemented in the manner that the plan defines.

Some religious orders have followed this approach and worked at producing a comprehensive plan, which typically contains a chapter on identity and mission, one which identifies key issues for ministry in the contemporary world, one on challenges to be faced by sections of the order, statistics on age and numbers and concrete action plans regarding apostolates to be undertaken. The provincial plays the leading role in the formulation and production of the plan. Then the plan is printed or published in a professional booklet and is promoted as the statement of who the order is and what it intends doing. This approach is useful and valuable once certain process issues are taken into consideration. One key issue is how what goes into the plan is created and formulated. If the members of the order are not ready for such a plan, then the emphasis must go into facilitating the kind of learning that needs to happen for the members to be able to move into the future in faith and consolation. Secondly, the perennial danger is that the production of the plan becomes more important than what is in it or what it is about. A focus on producing the plan may create rigidity and inflexibility – 'we can't do this because it is not in the plan'. Thirdly, the plan may be published too soon. The publication of the plan should be delayed until it is both well-understood and accepted and when its implementation is already well under way. Publishing a plan too soon or when it is not sufficiently well-understood and accepted may fail to generate the intended inspiration and not only fail to be the unifying force it aspires to be, but in fact be divisive and cause alienation.

The second approach might be termed the 'incremental' approach. In this approach strategy is emergent; it emerges out of the patterns of the past and becomes broad perspectives for the future, rather than as deliberate plans. In this approach there is no grand plan; decisions are made in an orderly manner out of what is happening and what has happened. Strategy emerges from the decisions made every day. Decision-making may appear to be piecemeal or disjointed.

There are different approaches to strategic planning, each with its own strengths and weaknesses.

This approach is frequently referred to as 'logical incrementalism' – there is a logic to the incremental decisions that are made. The problem with this approach can be that it can be disjointed, time-consuming and expensive in that resources may be invested in false starts or projects that don't turn out.

This approach is perhaps the most common in religious orders. Over the past twenty years, there have been chapters and many meetings which have followed different processes with facilitators and consultants. There have been workshops on community discernment, team-building, leadership and so on. There have been community and apostolic discernments. Over this period there is much that an order learns. Its members develop skills at facilitating groups, at spiritual direction, at discerning, at spiritual leadership. Decisions are made from time to time to opt for one ministry over another, to withdraw from a ministry, to open a new one. These do not happen in terms of a grand plan, but emerge as the right thing to do at a specific time. This approach is probably congruent with the culture of those orders which have a participative way of government and making decisions.

The third approach is the 'cultural' approach. This approach is fundamentally a process of collective behaviour based on beliefs shared by the organisation's members. This in effect means a shared belief system which is co-ordinated and controlled by the norms which are consistent with these shared beliefs. In other words, the beliefs are lived and are evident from patterns of decisions and actions.

The problem in this approach is that it does not encourage strategic change; rather it perpetuates existing strategy and consistency, emphasising tradition and consensus, it views change as complex and difficult and discourages strategic revolution, as for instance in bureaucracies whose stagnant cultures reinforce set procedures.

This approach to strategy is very applicable to religious life, which is based on strong ideology and culture. There are two perspectives on this approach. First, if the norms encourage the *status quo* and reinforce an unwillingness or inability to look at change, then stagnation does occur and ultimately, death. It

Having no strategy is itself a strategy.

becomes very difficult for a new provincial to change the culture and initiate change. The second perspective is that this approach to strategy is probably more aspired to than actually lived. It could best be summed up by the aspiration, 'discernment as a way of life'. A culture where it is the norm for the communities and apostolates to live a life of discernment, open to the voice of the Spirit in their experience, is espoused by many, if not all apostolic religious. As discussed elsewhere in this book, apostolic discernment in common depends on individual inner freedom as well as the ability of a group to create norms of group freedom, qualities which can be very difficult to create.

The point is that there are many approaches to strategy and each has its own strengths and weaknesses. Some approaches are formal and analytical. They believe in integrated decision-making, relying on analysis, formal planning and management control. Others are less formal and rely on political bargaining, consistency of behaviour – whether intended or unintended. Others place more emphasis on what emerges from past decisions, as distinct from a deliberate attempt to shape the future. Each approach has its strengths and weaknesses, and ultimately what any leadership needs to do is assess what the most appropriate approach is for a particular order/province at a given time. As movement into the future is unavoidable, it may be useful to note that strategy, strategic thinking and acting is also unavoidable. Just as doing nothing is actually doing something, having no strategy is itself a strategy!

APOSTOLIC REVIEW

Whatever the approach, planning still ends up in the realm of intention – what is desired. What is desired still has to be achieved, so plans have to be implemented. An over-emphasis on planning tends to neglect what is a more significant process, namely review. Review is the process whereby plans are examined, progress monitored and learning takes place. It may be analogous to particular individual review processes, such as the examen. Review may be perceived as a corporate apostolic examen.

A review process is aimed at facilitating learning from experience. Apostolic review can create a sense of guilt or defensiveness so easily when an atmosphere of psychological security and openness is absent. Accordingly, how review is structured is critical – when it takes place, in what context and how much time it is afforded. Holding an apostolic review when the provincial comes on visitation, that is, at a random time during the working year, may not facilitate the psychological space that an apostolic team may need in order to create the right atmosphere and dispositions in order to feel free to review an apostolate.

An over-emphasis on planning neglects review.

Discernment and review are critical at Levels I and II, that is at the individual and the team levels. Apostolic discernment in common and apostolic review in common are only possible when the individual is able to participate and is not dominated by pathologies which effectively block personal freedom. Discernment and review are key inter-level activities involving the individual and the team in such a way that the team review or discernment can only work if the individual is free.

DEFENSIVE REASONING AND ROUTINES

Chris Argyris, an eminent organisational psychologist, has devoted a good deal of his writings over the past twenty years to examining the basic assumptions under which organisations operate and how assumptions to deal with threat actually and unintentionally create patterns of defensive thinking and behaviour. Actions intended to increase understanding and trust often produce misunderstanding and mistrust. In Argyris' view, this is because individuals continually make inferences about others' motivations, don't test those inferences to see if they are accurate, and act on them as if they are true. Not only are these inferences undiscussable but having them is undiscussable also. I can withhold information from you on the assumption that if you find out you will be upset. I don't test that to see if it is true and I begin to take responsibility for your feelings. It is highly likely that you sense I am withholding something and make inferences about that. My action then has the opposite effect to what I am intending and sets up a defensive routine in which both you and I are equally implicated.

In applying the concept of defensive routines to the processes of strategic planning, Argyris poses the following seven questions:

1. Are there any problems with the planning process that you believe are critical but are not likely to be dealt with effectively?

2. What gets people in trouble when they deal with planning?

3. If you could change one thing in the planning process, what would it be? How would you go about doing it? What would you predict would be the biggest barrier to overcome?

4. If you could hang on to or strengthen a particular feature of the planning process, what would it be? How would you go about doing it? What would you predict would be the biggest barrier to overcome?

5. Are there any undiscussable or discussible but unchangeable issues in this organisation? Are any of these related to planning?

6. If there are none, what is it about this organisation that does not lead to undiscussable issues?

7. Recalling the defences that have been identified, how aware are people in this organisation that they exist? If they are aware, what leads them to continue? If they are not aware, what hunches do you have about the causes of their blindness?

What Argyris is getting at in these questions is uncovering the thinking that accompanies efforts at planning and change. When some individuals say things like, 'Nothing ever comes from these meetings', they are pointing to what they see to be errors in the system which they believe to be unchangeable. The next question would be, 'What in your judgement prevents anything happening out of these meetings?', the answer to which provides further insights into the defensive routines. A map of how defensive think-ing is created and how effective change is blocked can be developed and acted on.

Religious can collude very actively in processes which are unquest-ioned. Chapters are preceded by numerous questionnaires and sur-veys and followed up by an equal amount of reports and decrees. Reports and papers are distinguished by the colour of the paper on which they are printed. Community meetings can be devoted to issues which could be solved more appropriately by an individual. It can be assumed that in order to have effective consultation every member

> *A habit of not questioning assumptions can set up defensive routines*

of a community has to be consulted and so apostolic decision mak-ing becomes a tedious long-drawn out event as every member of the community, including those who are retired, express their view. It is not that any of the above examples are, of themselves, inappro-priate, but rather the effect they may be having in a group by not being brought into the open and examined for validity.

What may be problematic is that these activities may be defeating their very purpose. A consultation on an apostolic decision, which becomes embroiled in the fears and views of the elderly members of the community, gets bogged down in the unquestioned assumption that every one's opinion is of equal value. Accordingly, decision for the apostolate gets watered down to accommodate the anxieties of the elderly, and the active apostolic members of the ministry get frustrated and so the apostolate (which is the espoused priority) suffers. The coloured reports are not read which sets up the expect-ation that future ones will not be read either, while yet the papers continue to be circulated and a routine of covering up the senseless-ness of the procedures ensues.

CONCLUSIONS

This chapter has reflected on strategy in the process of managing planned change. The five 'Ps' – plan, ploy, pattern, position and perspective – provide a useful map of how strategy might be approached. Strategy was defined in terms of its four elements – core mission, environmental scan, internal review and strategic posture. Some approaches to forming strategy were articulated, with particular emphasis on distinguishing between a formal, explicit design approach and an incrementalist, piecemeal approach. Both approaches are valid and each has its own strengths and weaknesses. An approach to strategy needs to be evaluated, whatever the model, remembering that an emergent strategy can as easily be unintended as intended. A note was sounded to remind that planning is always in the realm of intention and desires and that the implementation of plans must be reviewed. Apostolic review is that process whereby what is being learned from the experience of planning and implementing plans is explicitated and acted on. Finally, a habit of not questioning assumptions and practices can lead to routines being set up which inhibit learning.

CHAPTER 3

Strategic Leadership

Leadership is a complex subject to talk about and understand. It is said that it is the most researched and written about subject in the social sciences. Part of the complexity of looking at it in an organisational context is that leadership occurs throughout a system. It exists in the formal hierarchical roles of an organisation, such as in supervisors, managers, administrators, provincials, superiors and principals. It exists in the informal organisation where individuals, who have no formal rank, generate ideas, lead groups, get things done and so on. Such a perspective entices one to look at the groups in which leadership occurs and conclude that leadership must be viewed in the context of the group within which it occurs.

The context of religious apostolic leadership has changed a lot over the past thirty years. Thirty years ago, religious had a very definite predominance in institutions of ministry. They were dominant numerically. They were the sole formulators of policy. They created the culture of the institutions. Leadership was exercised in an autocratic manner that did not readily allow for question or dissent. Since Vatican II there has been a gradual change. Religious life has been renewed, in terms of spirituality, structures and culture. The number of religious has declined, changing the way religious are present in their ministries and provoking questions about the future of particular ministries. On the level of values, there has been the growth in an appreciation of the ministry of the laity. Overall there has grown a new focus of ministry – evangelisation – with its encouragement of a greater openness to the contemporary world and the articulation of the integral relationship between faith and justice. Leadership too has changed. In research on leadership there has been a movement away from a focus on the person of the leader toward a focus on the process of leadership. Leadership is no longer understood in terms of personal traits but in terms of a process between roles, a group and a situation. In the religious life context terms like 'co-operation', 'sharing ministry' are prominent. Decision-making has moved towards becoming a group activity, with, perhaps, the consequent role of the formal leader sometimes ambiguous. There is a search for a reformulation of the nature of leadership in religious life, with a dissatisfaction with terms like superior, provincial and general. There is an emphasis on leadership, animation, facilitation, empowering and so on. This chapter focuses on one particular formal leader, the major superior (regional superior, provincial, general or whatever the term is within whatever structure) with regard to the strategic process. Leaders have to balance and integrate the levels of organisation presented in chapter 1. They have responsibilities to God's people through individuals (Level I), ministries and communities (Level II), the province or region as a whole (Level III), the congregation and its charism (Level IV) and then to the wider church through the bishops and conference of religious (Level V).

In terms of the formal role, leadership is not the same as administration or management. It is common to say that so and so is a good administrator but not a good leader or vice versa. Management and

> *Leadership is an ability to inspire people, build commitment and lead change.*

administration tend to be defined as a role which helps keep an operation functioning – getting the jobs done and so on. Leadership, on the other hand, is typically defined in terms of an ability to inspire people, build commitment and lead change. An individual may be very efficient and administer well but not have the interpersonal qualities of a leader, just as an inspirational leader may not be a good administrator. Much of the preoccupation which many religious have with the subject of local leadership is often a concern about local administration.

CO-OPERATIVE LEADERSHIP

The cultural emphasis on co-operative leadership is not confined to the church or religious contexts. In many organisations the challenge of attempting to maintain quality with reduced resources, the expectations of shared power and responsibility, an increase in interdependence and communication, the need for more people in problem-solving because of increasing complexity, are some of the trends that have been identified as greatly affecting the role require-ments of leaders and followers in organisations. These changes in role requirements affect both leaders and followers.

Leaders need to unlearn traditional leadership orientations, such as the model of vertical authority and dependence and the assump-tion that 'doing it by yourself' is a sign of strength. A change from pride in independence and autonomy, to pride in interdependence and mutual help, can be difficult. The challenges for leaders in this contemporary culture are described in terms of attitudes and skills for change, an ability to mobilise resources for themselves and so reduce stress, an achievement of an integration of centralised and decentralised decision-making, an effective interdependence between focus on task and process, team-building with diverse people, and an ability to use outside resources.

Followers too must adapt their attitudes, roles and skills to comple-ment a different approach to leadership. Followers need to be less passive and reactive as members. The discrepancies between what is and what ought to be can result in fault finding and withdrawal from participation. Members have a key responsibility to shape leadership. They need to learn how to influence upwards so that leaders will listen attentively.

The co-operative model requires a renewal of both leaders and fol-lowers. There is a new pattern of relationship. Leadership training, which focused on strengthening the role of the leader without an equivalent focus on strengthening the skills of the followers, is seen as inadequate. The emphasis now is on training the group to develop the skills of collaboration. The frequency of workshops and semi-nars on group skills, an emphasis on process, team-building, to take a few examples, are manifestations of how these skills are being developed.

LEADERSHIP AND CULTURE

Organisational culture is defined as, 'a pattern of basic assumptions – invented, discovered, or developed by a given group as it learns to cope with its problems of external adaptation and internal integ-ration – that has worked well enough to be considered valid and, therefore, to be taught to new members as the correct way to perceive, think, and feel in relation to those problems' (Schein, 1992, p. 17). There are three levels of organisational culture, the artefact level, the values level, and the basic assumptions level. The artefact level is found in what is visible and overt. Religious living in big houses behind high walls or living in apartments among the poor are examples of signs of different cultures. Underlying these observable signs and behaviours are values. The values should be the predictors of behaviour. In this sense values are a deeper level of culture than what is observable. We know, of course, that what are espoused as values are not always depicted in behaviour. There can often be an inconsistency between what is espoused and what in fact is operative. The third level of culture is that of basic assumptions. Basic assumptions are the unexamined rationale of attitudes and behaviour which have been handed on to us by others, which we have internalised and taken for granted and so don't notice them any more. Uncovering what basic assumptions underlying what is actually happening is difficult because these assumptions are taken for granted and implicit. Often it takes an outsider to piece together the patterns of behaviour and question the assumptions.

Organisational leaders are primary agents in creating, embedding and forming cultural assumptions. What particular organisational leaders pay attention to, measure and control, how they react to critical incidents and organisational crises, how they are role models, what they reward, are some instances of how leader play a central role in the formation of culture. The way the organisation is designed in terms of structure and procedures is

Leaders are primary agents in creating culture.

another mechanism for reinforcing cultural assumptions. In the model of religious life prior to Vatican II, there were very clear visible structures. The lives of individuals were tightly controlled. Permissions were required for almost everything. The values behind those structures were articulated in terms of total commitment, self-abandonment to God's will, community formation. The deeper assumptions operative were about the nature of the person and the nature of grace. There has been a change since Vatican II. The structures and behaviours have changed. The values have changed, as too have many of the basic assumptions. The point here is that leaders play a key role in the formation of culture. In the way that they actually behave – what they are seen to value – they are significant in embedding culture in an organisation. When a person in a leadership position cancels planning meetings to visit the sick, for example, that may give a message that planning may be less important.

THE LEADERSHIP GRID®

Provincials frequently present their leadership dilemmas in terms of a tension between the apostolate of the group and the individual. They find, in some cases, that a beneficial situation for one excludes the benefit of the other. This is undoubtedly true in some instances. As provincials tend to have a responsibility for both as part of the description of their role, a framework which takes account of both is useful.

Robert Blake and Jane Mouton developed a framework for understanding and evaluating human effectiveness and leadership over thirty years ago. This framework, called the Grid, has been refined and developed over that period. In its essence, the Grid charts a range of behavioural choices along a three dimensional figure. The horizontal axis shows a concern for outcome or results on a scale of 1 to 9. An individual leader may be high (a score of 9), low (a score of 1), or in the middle (a score of 5), on this concern for outcome. On the vertical axis, which shows a concern for people on a scale of 1 to 9, an individual leader may be high (a score of 9), low (a score of 1), or in the middle (a score of 5), on concern for people. Of course, religious leaders are 'expected' to have a high concern for people. However, we know from experience that this is not always borne out in behaviour. Putting these horizontal and vertical axes together gives a two dimensional grid with seven points plotted on it (Figure 3-1, overleaf). Each point may be viewed as a Grid style.

While the two concerns may be viewed as independent, they actually merge when forming a Grid style. When individuals work with others on a task, the concerns become interdependent. They may be compared to ingredients in making a cake. Ingredients, such as flour and sugar, exist independently but in being mixed and baked, they merge to help form a cake. In Grid terms, this interdependence can be explained through the following example. If the following

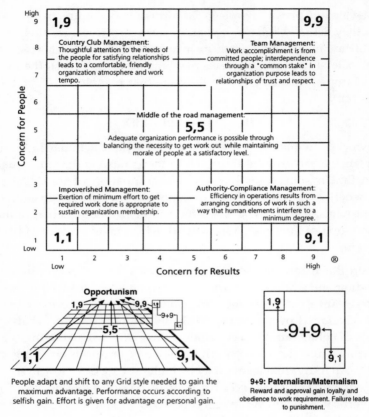

People adapt and shift to any Grid style needed to gain the maximum advantage. Performance occurs according to selfish gain. Effort is given for advantage or personal gain.

9+9: Paternalism/Maternalism
Reward and approval gain loyalty and obedience to work requirement. Failure leads to punishment.

Source:
The Leadership Grid® figure, Paternalism Figure and Opportunism from *Leadership Dilemmas--Grid Solutions*, by Robert R. Blake and Anne Adams McCanse (Formerly the Managerial Grid by Robert R. Blake and Jane S. Mouton). Houston: Gulf Publishing Company, (Grid Figure: P. 29, Paternalism Figure: p. 30, Opportunism Figure: p. 31). Copyright 1991 by Scientific Methods, Inc. Reproduced by permission of the owners.

Figure 3-1
The Leadership Grid Figure

high concern for outcome, 'I exert vigorous effort to achieve outcomes', stands alone, it doesn't say much about how I work with others. However, if I say, 'I exert vigorous effort to achieve outcomes and force others to comply' then I am illustrating that my high concern for outcomes (9) is joined by a low concern for people (1). On the other hand, my high concern for outcome may be 'I exert vigorous effort to achieve outcomes and others work with me enthusiastically'. Then, in this instance, my high concern for outcome (9) is accompanied by a high concern for people (9).

There is a third dimension which is a motivational scale on which is plotted something of the range of reasons why people operate out of a particular Grid style, ranging from the '+' end of seeking something which the leader wants or needs to the '-' end which reflects something the leader wants to avoid. This third dimension pro-

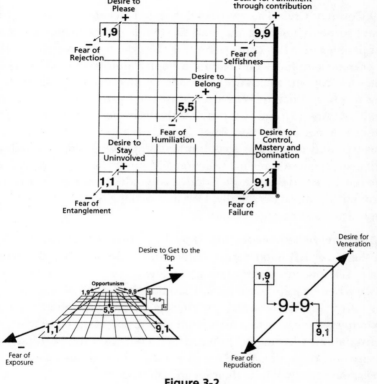

Figure 3-2
Positive and Negative Motivations

vides a framework for reflecting on and understanding personal motivations. The motivational scale points to motivations which exist in any Grid style (Figure 3-2).

9,1 Authority-Obedience The 9,1, oriented style is located at the lower right hand corner of the Grid, and marks a style which has a high concern for task, with people's needs receiving low concern. Provincials' emphasis is on efficiency and results, with members of the province expected to carry out their commands. Why do 9,1 leaders act this way? At one extreme of the motivational scale is a desire for mastery and control, and at the other a fear of failure. 9,1 oriented provincials control authorisation, are hard driving, distrustful, find fault and make all the decisions. Conflict is perceived as a threat to authority.

1,9 Country Club The 1,9 oriented style is located at the top left hand corner of the Grid and marks a style which has a high concern for people and a low concern for task. 1,9 oriented provincials place a primary emphasis on creating a happy atmosphere where people's feelings and needs are catered for, with outcome needs receiving a lower concern. Why do 1,9 oriented provincials act in this way? At one extreme 1,9 provincials desire to please, and at the other is a fear of rejection. They feel secure when relationships are positive and others are accepting and approving, while avoiding criticism because it means rejection and hurt. They cannot say No, are sensitive and easily hurt. Conflict is avoided because 1,9 oriented provincials take it personally. Decision-making is nice when people embrace it and engage in sharing.

1,1 Impoverished Leadership The 1,1 oriented Grid style is located at the lower left hand corner of the Grid and marks a style where there is a low concern for task and a low concern for people. It is a style whereby individual provincials have opted out of responsibility. Why do 1,1 oriented provincials behave like this? At one extreme is the desire to remain uninvolved, and at the other a fear of termination. 1,1 oriented provincials do not want the position and so are noncommittal, avoid conflict and go through the motions. At the same time they hide their feelings of discontent and do not face up to their desires not to have the responsibility. Sometimes this style can be associated with ill-health or impending retirement.

5,5 Middle of the Road The 5,5 oriented Grid style is located at the centre of the Grid and marks a compromise position of balancing the two concerns. 5,5 oriented provincials are motivated by a desire to belong, on the one hand, and a fear of humiliation on the other. Accordingly, they set a middle path of accommodation, not rocking the boat, going with the majority, following precedent and tradition and trying to keep everyone happy.

9,9 Team Leadership The 9,9 oriented Grid style is located at the top right hand corner of the Grid and marks an integrated high concern for task and for people, with which there is no contradiction. This does not mean that everyone gets what they want or that they agree with the final decision, but that they are involved in the process, feel heard, understand what is happening and why. Thus there is commitment. 9,9 oriented provincials are motivated by a desire for fulfilment through contribution, on the one hand, and a fear of selfishness which loses the contribution of others on the other. 9,9 oriented provincials see conflict as good as it brings the issues into the open, and so work to solve them directly with understanding and agreement. 9,9 oriented provincials build commitment around vision, standards of excellence, clear expectations, shared values, and participation in problem-solving and decision-making. This does not mean that everyone is always involved in every decision. The underlying principle is that each is responsible for their own actions and that people can learn from reflecting on experience. When a group is engaging in communal or corporate discernment, 9,9 behaviour is required, as discernment in common requires careful and sensitive attention to the issue under consideration and to how the participants in the discernment feel about it.

9+9 Paternalist/Maternalist Leadership The 9+9 oriented Grid style is a combination of 1,9 and 9,1, where there is a simultaneous high concern for task and people but they are not integrated. Paternalism or maternalism portrays behaviour from the two styles in a way which utilises reward and punishment. The high 9 of concern for people is contingent on the other person's compliance and support. Paternalistic provincials are parental figures, benevolent autocrats, dispensing approval and disapproval and demanding loyalty. Why do 9+9 oriented provincials act in this way? At one extreme there is the desire for veneration and, at the other, the fear of repudiation. Paternalist provincials enjoy admiration, giving advice and approval and having others emulate them as models. They are hurt when their advice is ignored and are blind to any smothering effect their behaviour might be having. They may induce guilt through condescending behaviour which stunts growth in others. They are the sole decision maker and decisions are made for the good of others. Any consultation is an illusion.

Opportunistic Opportunist provincials use the combination of the other Grid styles on the basis of what is likely to help them get ahead. In their dealing with others, they are working from the question of what Grid style is likely to help them get what they want from the other person. Opportunistic oriented behaviour is rooted in self interest. Why do opportunistic provincials act in this way? At one extreme is the desire to be in control, and on the other a fear of exposure.

Grid Style Consistency and Flexibility

There is a Grid style consistency in that people tend to deal with others in more or less the same way, even over long periods. Despite this relative consistency, there are exceptions in which people may switch temporarily from one style to another before returning to their typical style of relating.

> *There is Grid Style consistency in that people tend to deal with others in more or less the same way.*

The stable mode of relating is referred to as the *dominant style* and the flexibility of shifting to another style is referred to as a *backup style*. The shift to backup style is spontaneous, frequently in situations of crisis, stress, conflict or new environments.

The dominant style is the one most characteristic of people, the one you know and anticipate of them. With the exception of opportunism, each of the six leadership styles is relatively consistent, regardless of the situation or people involved. Some may think that Grid styles don't work when a crisis arises, but most leaders don't pick and choose an approach each time they are faced with a new situation. They respond in a instinctive way to questions, decisions, conflicts and so on. The approach reflects the individual's motivations, past experiences, feelings, values and desires.

In some situations, when a dominant style isn't effective, a person may shift temporarily to a backup style. For example, mild-mannered 1,9 oriented leaders may suddenly lose their temper and shout at someone. The sudden change probably shocks both parties. The leader will most likely return to the dominant style when the temporary circumstances pass, with an apology and explanation for the unusual behaviour. There are times when leaders give up, get annoyed, patronise and so on, especially when they don't feel they have the energy to keep listening and helping an individual. While leaders may have clear 9,9 desires about what they want to achieve, their own frailty and lack of skill means that they don't always live that out. A more serious reason may be a lack of self-awareness as to their motivations; hence, the motivational scale attached to each behavioural style. Therefore, an important area of learning for leaders is their self-awareness of what their dominant and backup styles are and developing skills in working with others to achieve desired outcomes.

Grid style is not about what leaders do, but is about how they do it.

ELEMENT	DESCRIPTION
Initiative	Exercising effort, drive and support for specific activities.
Inquiry	Questioning, seeking information, and testing for understanding of possible actions.
Advocacy	Expressing attitudes, opinions, ideas and convictions regarding an activity.
Decision Making	Considering alternative possibilities to establish a course of action.
Resilience	Reacting to outcomes as they influence the ability to move forward.
Conflict Resolution	How feelings of disagreement are expressed in dealing with others.
Critique	Learning through studying and comparing yours and other's values, attitudes and emotions toward resolving conflict.

Table 3-1
Leadership Grid
Elements of Communication

In the concrete day-to-day tasks of dealing with people, key areas of communication are: initiative, inquiry, advocating one's own position, reacting to problems, making decisions, handling conflict and reflecting on experience with others (Table 3-1). A clear understanding of the Grid helps people communicate more effectively and work together to achieve common tasks.

The Grid approach to understanding leadership behaviour is more fully developed in the texts referenced at the end of this book. It is the strategic leadership context that warrants further attention here.

STRATEGIC LEADERSHIP

Corporate leaders are said to perform three roles: organisational leader, personal leader and architect of purpose. Leaders are 'organisational leaders', by which is meant that they lead the organisation in a general management role. This typically involves being responsible for the accomplishment of the organisation's stated plans. It means creatively maintaining and developing the organisation's capabilities in its external and internal domains so that achieve-

Corporate leaders are 'organisational leaders', 'personal leaders', 'architects of purpose'.

ment of its tasks are possible. Organisational leaders integrate the multiple functions and specialist areas within the organisation. These are complex tasks and require all the qualities of effectiveness that are accepted as being a core ingredient of a senior management role. Secondly, leaders are 'personal leaders' whereby they are leaders of people. They must be personally able to create loyalty. They personally stand for and promote the values of the organisation and so their actions must be congruent with those values. It is their behaviour as leader that forms the culture of the organisation. Thirdly, leaders are 'architects of purpose'. In this role they are custodians of corporate objectives, establishing and presiding over the setting of goals and the allocation of resources, and making choices from strategic alternatives. They defend the organisation from external threats and internal erosion. The installation of purpose in place of improvisation and the substitution of planned progress instead of drifting are leaders' most demanding tasks. It requires great intellectual capacity to conceptualise corporate purpose and creativity to recognise strategic alternatives. It requires a critical capacity to analyse the strengths and weaknesses of proposals on paper.

There is a parallel in relation to religious apostolic leadership. Provincials have those same roles. They are organisational leaders, personal leaders and architects of purpose. They are entrusted with the effective administration of their province. The organisational leader role is exercised in the day-to-day desk work, the eternal round of meetings and reports, all working to keeping the province in operation and fulfiling its mission. As personal leader, there is the maintenance of the charism and values of the congregation. The personal care of one's fellow religious is a key responsibility of provincials. As architects of purpose, provincials integrate the processes of planning and renewal in terms of the congregation's charism, the needs of the external environment and the internal resources. It involves going beyond the immediate and everyday decisions and emergencies to thinking strategically about a future to be created.

Provincials, like all corporate leaders, live in two time zones. As organisational leaders and personal leaders they live in the present; as architects of purpose they live in the future, having a sense of vision and purpose about where they want to lead the province. The exercise of the three leadership roles requires a dual concern for the apostolate and for the people working in it. Architect of purpose has a specific focus, namely the leadership of the province into the future. This focus is referred to as a strategic focus and requires provincials to think and act strategically.

The principles of Grid leadership are directly played out in the three roles of the provincial as corporate leader. As personal and organisational leaders, provincials engage the members of the province in their living out of the mission of the congregation. While provincials

> *The role of 'architect of purpose' requires provincials to think and act strategically.*

are required, in theory, to exhibit 9,9 behaviour towards each individual member of the province, this does not always happen. Provincials may have opted out with respect to some individuals (1,1). They may not want to upset some individuals and so placate them to keep the peace (1,9). They may settle for compromise with other individuals (5,5). In some instances it may be that they behave in a directive manner and do not listen to the individual (9,1) or work from the premise that they know what is best for an individual (9+9). As already emphasised, these behaviours may be consequent on a lack of energy in a demanding role, a lack of skill in dealing with some situations, or a lack of self-awareness.

It is with respect to the role of architect of purpose that the Grid styles also apply. 9,1 oriented provincials make plans and decisions without engaging members of the province or listening to their views. 9+9 oriented provincials know what is best for the province and direct it in the direction that they have decided, while attempting to convince the members that this is the best way. 1,9 oriented provincials don't make plans because they are unwilling to upset some members of the province, perhaps the elderly. 1,1 oriented provincials do not engage in the strategic process at all and leave it to their successors. 5,5 oriented provincials maintain the *status quo* as much as possible, do some planning and make some decisions but essentially keep the balance of the *status quo*.

9,9 oriented provincials help articulate a vision and facilitate and enable members of the province to engage in it. They can move ahead and not be paralysed by people's anxieties and fears. They confront into the issues directly while facilitating members of the province to face their anxieties and move towards commitment to decisions. Corporate discernment and decision making are central processes for 9,9 oriented provincial.

Effective leadership is key to large-scale organisational change. Following on from what was discussed in chapter 2, we can see that provincials have to make choices about what strategic approach to take. One may follow an incremental linear approach where decisions are made in sequence over time. Priorities are reflected in the decisions which are made from month to month, year to year and which find expression in the allocation of personnel and finance. Members of a province may see that because a particular school has received younger personnel and other resources, it has a priority over other schools which have not received equivalent resources. A second approach follows a more fundamental, systemic change approach whereby a change strategy, through which the whole system will change simultaneously, is adopted. Such an approach involves having a vision of a desired end state which guides the analysis of the need for change and the change process itself. This will be developed more in chapter 5.

The person in the leadership position, provincial and council or team, must be committed champions of the change. A description of the changed state provides a focus and direction for the process and creates conditions that preclude maintenance of the *status quo*. As we will see in chapter 5, this involves attention to process as well as content. It involves working with and across the four levels so that individuals, teams and communities, the balance of ministries in a province, are affected by the strategic action in harmony with the charism of the order.

CONCLUSIONS

Leadership is one of the most researched and written-about topics in the social sciences. It has received its share of attention in the religious renewal literature since Vatican II. Contemporary leadership writing focuses on the ability to inspire vision to create the future, to influence through relationship and to call the group into prayerful searching for the way forward. The Grid framework has been used to lay out the concrete dimensions of leading apostolic endeavours and attending to the needs of individuals. As architects of purpose, provincials must manage this tension and maintain the integrity of their responsibility, so that there is a future for the living charism of the order.

Managing Change and Renewal

The management of change has become one of the most vital issues in organisational life in this latter part of the twentieth century. Change keeps coming. The old order of a period of stability being disrupted and causing some change, which is then followed by a period of stability, no longer holds. There is such a lack of certainty that change has to be conceived in discontinuous terms. Religious orders have not been exempt from this issue. Apostolic ministries of all kinds have faced and are facing change. Religious orders in their internal forum are grappling with change. In some instances change is voluntary. Frequently it is forced from outside. The call in Vatican II to 'read the signs of the times and interpret them in the light of the gospel' has inspired reformulations of charism in contemporary terms and affected the kinds of ministry and the ways in which ministry is exercised. Internally, religious orders have shrunk in size making reorganisation of ministry mandatory. For effective management of change, religious orders and ministries need to be clear about their mission and future vision, read and interpret the signs of the times, and adapt internally to the goals that emerge from the analysis in the light of charism.

There are many tasks in the change process. Some tasks require careful evaluation of the present situation. Other tasks emphasise the desired future. A third group of tasks demand that the transition from the present to the future be well-managed. This section attempts to articulate some of the issues and processes in these three groups of tasks, and emphasises the need for a systematic approach to the complex issue of planned change.

ORGANISATION DEVELOPMENT

Organisation development (OD) is an approach to the management of organisational change. It is not always easy to explain what it is because the field is still being shaped by its practitioners and theorists. One of the best known definitions, by French and Bell is:

> Organisation development is a top-management-supported, long range effort to improve the organisation's problem-solving and renewal processes, particularly through a more effective and collaborative diagnosis and management of organisational culture – with special emphasis on formal work team, temporary team, and intergroup culture, with the assistance of a consultant-facilitator and the use of theory and technology of applied behavioural science, including action research (p. 17).

The above definition provides something of the flavour of OD. The common elements in this and other definitions focus on long-term organisational change, supported by top leadership, using behavioural science in a manner that enables the organisation to learn about itself and develop change skills.

This, in effect, means establishing the kinds of organisational conditions whereby a religious order or apostolic ministry can develop a self-renewing system in which there is a unified sense of charism, an agreed analysis of the external needs to which the order is called to respond in the light of its charism, and the application of such organisational tools as planning and the mobilisation of financial and personnel resources to generate appropriate apostolic action. Renewal of this depth and magnitude has profound implications for the order's culture, communication patterns, community life, formation and leadership. Typically, OD intervenes in those dimensions. It focuses on leadership, external adaptation, problem-solving, decision-making, structures, planning, cultural norms, roles, communication, team relations, inter-group relations, training and conflict management. OD is, of necessity, a long-term effort that is intimately related to the order's mission. It is action-oriented and frequently involves experienced-based learning. It frequently assumes that groups and teams are the basic units for organisational change.

Organisation development is both an underlying philosophy of bringing about change and a whole range of techniques. As a philosophy it is grounded in such assumptions as: (a) that change involves unlearning attitudes and habits which are already well imbedded and integrated in existing behaviours and social relationships; (b) that change will not take place unless there is some motivation to change, and that creating the motivation to change is often the most difficult part of the change process; and (c) that while it is the individual who ultimately changes and mediates change in an organisation, the groups to which individuals belong, and with which they identify, are the key focus and agents of change.

ACTION RESEARCH

Alfred Marrow, Lewin's biographer, called Lewin 'the practical theorist', a term which neatly sums up the thrust of Lewin's work. Lewin blended experimentation with theory and viewed social science as the study of real problems. Accordingly, he connected problem solving with theory and defined theory in terms of action. The term 'action research' can be applied to mean many forms of research, but its core meaning refers to a way of involving participants in a social system in collecting data about themselves and then using the data to take some remedial or developmental action. Organisation development grew out of an approach to learning in small groups which took place by the individuals attending to the here and now situation which was occurring in the group. This was an insight which Lewin got and which his colleagues developed by setting up unstructured group situations which had the aim of helping the participants learn about groups. In these groups (called T-groups, T standing for training) the emphasis was on participants acting as the active agents of their own change by participating in the group, reflecting on what was happening, understanding their experience in the light of behavioural science constructs and then attempting to adapt their behaviour to accord with their insights about themselves. The trainer's non-directive, facilitative role enables the participants to take control of their own learning. (Later the insights of the T-group were adopted by Carl Rogers and the emphasis was shifted to focus on the individual's personal development. Thus sensitivity groups were created.) In the T-group the emphasis was on group-skills development learning. It was when the core insights of the T-group were developed to deal with task issues in working groups and to work in larger systems that OD emerged. In organisation development, the consultant works in a facilitative manner, enabling the members of the organisation do their own analysis of what their problems are, create their own solutions to these problems, implement their solutions and reflect on the consequences, both intended and unintended.

Organisation development itself is the fruit of action research – a philosophy of how to be helpful to client systems by working with them to understand what is going on and how to help change happen. Each step in the change process, each intervention, creates new information which must be understood to try to see what the next step might be, and so on. Through OD an organisation is not only changing but also learning about change and learning to learn about change.

Organisation development is very compatible with, and in many ways, ideally suited to the renewal process in religious life. Its approach to how people learn, how people make decisions and the function of groups as key to organisational change, blend well with the structure and culture of religious life. The spirituality of reflecting on experience in the light of desires and decisions can avail of organisation development's emphasis on process and focus on what is appropriate to the way an organisation makes decisions and manages change.

Structure of Part 2

Part 2 contains six chapters. Chapter 4 presents a generic change model which identifies three issues and stages of change – being motivated to change, changing and making the change work and survive. Chapter 5 describes the processes whereby a complex system changes. Chapter 6 shows that, because everyone does not change at the same time, there is a time and energy sequence which is also critical to the process of change. Chapter 7 emphasises the key role groups such as task forces and commissions play in the change process, and argues for an approach to working in such groups which focuses on learning. Chapter 8 describes the nature and dynamics of assemblies. Chapter 9 introduces the role of the external helper, describes different models of helping, and distinguishes between consultation and facilitation.

CHAPTER 4

Understanding Change

One important element in understanding the change process is to understand that change is equivalent to re-education. In other words, something has to be unlearned and be replaced by new attitudes or behaviours. It is generally recognised that the process of re-education is more complex than that of education. It is easier to learn something for the first time than to re-adapt one's habits in order to learn new ones.

Kurt Lewin, the eminent social psychologist, spent a great deal of his life studying how habits are changed and he formulated the process of re-education in a number of principles. In Lewin's view, effective re-education affects the individual in three ways: thought structures, values and beliefs, and behaviour. He noted that in re-education, direct experiencing alone does not bring about learning or change. People can persist in the same behaviour, even though it may have ceased to be useful. Experiencing has to be integrated with theory so that there is understanding of what happens. Theory alone does not suffice to bring about changes in feelings, rather it can heighten the gap between the official system of values and what the individual really feels.

For Lewin, the manner in which change is introduced is important in order to avoid any polarisation between loyalty to an old value system and hostility to a new, so as to ensure the individual has freedom to choose. The paradox between insisting on the freedom of the individual to change and the necessity of having to provoke change is answered in two ways by Lewin. First, change does not come about by logically arguing item by item; that approach tends to drive the individual into a corner. Any approach to re-education needs to have an overall strategy. Second, accepting new values and beliefs comes about for the individual by membership of a group, which accepts the new values.

Complementing his work on re-education, Lewin developed three
stages of a change process out of his research into changing eating
habits in Iowa during the second world war. The first stage he
called the 'unfreezing' stage. In this
stage, the motivation to change is
created. There are typically four
sources of unfreezing. There can be
an experience of pain or dissatisfac-
tion with a present situation, so the driving force for change can be
a desire for relief. The dissatisfaction can be from a perceived dis-
crepancy between what is and what ought to be. There can be external pressures to change. The move to change can arise from the
internal thrust towards wholeness or health.

> *Change involves 'unfreezing'*
> *from the old state, 'moving' to*
> *the new state, and 'refreezing'*
> *in the new state.*

Lewin's model was developed by Edgar Schein who specified the
dynamics within each stage. Schein identified three mechanisms
which must be operating in order for the individual to feel motivated
to change.

i) Present behaviour or attitudes must be disconfirmed.

ii) The disconfirmation must arouse sufficient anxiety or guilt to
actually create change.

iii) Sufficient 'psychological safety' is provided to make it
unnecessary for the target individuals or teams to psychologically defend themselves because the disconfirming information
is too threatening or the anxiety or guilt are too high.

The unfreezing process is painful and generates a number of specific
psychological responses such as denial and dodging. When experience is disconfirmed, the initial reaction is to deny the relevance of
the disconfirming information. When the evidence supporting
change is unsustainable then it can be dodged – others have to
change, not me. Effective unfreezing involves a recognition of the
need for change in such a form that there is a balance of the pain of
the disconfirmation with the assurance that change is possible and
can be undertaken with some personal safety. There may be a time
delay between disconfirmation and a sense of psychological safety.
An individual may perceive the need for change and feel the need
to do something about it, but may not feel secure enough to act at
the moment. The unfreezing process may take a considerable

amount of time and energy, but it is essential if any change is to take place. When there is a lack of attention to unfreezing, i.e. when the motivation and desire for change is neglected, then there is typically coercion for change. Those who are 'unfrozen' pressurise those who are not. This increases resistance. While resistance is an inherent element in change, forces which increase resistance are unhelpful. They generate energy into issues that are not central to the change. Lewin found that interventions to help reduce resistance, rather than to increase the drive for change, were more productive. Attention to the unfreezing stage is critical because if there is no felt-need for change then any efforts will meet with resistance.

In Schein's view, what is critical and typically neglected in the above process, with respect to organisational learning and change, is that of creating psychological safety. Disconfirmation is prevalent; it is always easy to show what is wrong and what needs improving or changing. It is relatively easy to create guilt or anxiety about the consequences of not changing. What is necessary, in Schein's view, is that if organisations are to learn how to learn and change often (as they need to do in the contemporary world) they need to be able to speed up the process and not get bogged down in the anxieties which inhibit learning and change and which tend to be increased when there is an emphasis on disconfirmation and the consequences of not changing. Accordingly, creating psychological safety and reducing the debilitating elements of anxiety are critical. The role played by any one in a helping function, such as a consultant, is one which must be sensitive to and facilitative of these complex psychological processes involved in learning and changing, as they frequently inhibit learning and change. Such a facilitative role is the essence of organisation development as an approach to learning and change.

There are many disconfirming forces for religious orders. There are the changes in society which are taking place – secularisation, decline of the family, increasing poverty and the growing gap between rich and poor, to cite some obvious examples. There is the changing nature of our understanding of church, with the growing emphasis on the apostolate of the laity. Internally, there are falling numbers of vocations and a preponderance of ageing members. For some, these disconfirming forces are the source of much psychological anxiety and provide a sense of loss for a former way of life; for others it is a challenge and an opportunity to move into new areas and develop new forms of ministry and community living.

The second stage is the 'moving/changing' stage. Here, the focus is on developing alternatives to the old situation, through generating new information and new ways of looking at the old situation. Schein calls this process 'cognitive redefinition'. This is the stage most commonly thought of as the change process. Experimentation is normative in the search for new solutions. This process occurs through one of two mechanisms. First, there is the process of identification, whereby learning occurs through experiencing things from another person's point of view and using that person as a role model for one's own behaviour. This is the change mechanism inherent through the use of a consultant, therapist, spiritual director, mentor or friend. Secondly, there is the process of scanning the environment for information relevant to one's particular problems and selecting solutions from multiple sources. Unless there is already real motivation to change, these activities will be fruitless exercises.

The third stage is what Lewin calls the 'refreezing' stage. This is an often ill-defined stage but is critical to change. It involves stabilising the new normative pattern of behaviour. Many individuals, groups and organisations undergo a change process only to revert to the old pattern some time later. This third stage aims at integrating the change into the new pattern so that it survives. The refreezing stage is defined in terms of the change's integration into the normative pattern of behaviour. It requires conscious management, typically in the form of institutionalisation processes. Two mechanisms are essential. The changed state must be experienced as fitting the self-concept (what Schein calls 'personal refreezing'), and there must be some forms of social support, whereby maintaining the new behaviour is rewarded (what Schein calls 'relational refreezing'). This new state remains in a semi-permanent position till it is unfrozen by new requirements for change.

CHANGE AGENTS

Those who help change to enter and take root in a system can be understood as 'change agents'. Change agent activity occurs on

Lewin's three stages of change. There are those who help an organisation unfreeze. These are 'change generators' and are those who generate the need for change. Examples of change generators are those who perceive a need for change and agitate for it or support it. 'Change implementors' are those who help the change happen in the system. Examples include superiors and external consultants and facilitators. Those who help stabilise the change are 'change adopters'.

For change to move through a complex system like a religious order, all three roles are necessary. Ideas put forward by inspirational people who push for change must be taken up at some stage by superiors (perhaps helped by consultants) and established in the system. Ultimately they have to be followed through by a substantive number of members for the change to survive. So every change process requires generators, implementors and adopters. How these roles interact, and how the change agenda advances or is frustrated, depends on the management of the change process.

FOUR PSYCHOLOGICAL REACTIONS TO CHANGE

Change involves a letting go in order to move on, a dying and resurrection. Accordingly, the unfreezing process may be painful and contain a number of specific psychological responses which need to be analysed. So further articulation of the elements within disconfirmation and the creation of psychological safety is useful. When we

> *Change involves letting go in order to move on, a dying and resurrection.*

look at change in large systems, such as an organisation or a religious order, we notice that the movement from unfreezing through changing to refreezing actually involves a complex journey through the four organisational levels as individuals, teams and communities, and a province change. In the remainder of this chapter a description of four psychological stages of change – denying, dodging, doing and sustaining – will be developed, and in chapter 6 applied to how these stages interconnect with the four levels in a seven-phase change process.

First Stage: Denying

The denial stage begins when the data supporting a change are first brought into the organisation, i.e. when disconfirmation first starts.

It can be a denial of the need for change in the face of others' assertion of the need to change or a need for change caused by environmental forces. This stage centres round processing information, disputing its value, relevance or timeliness. The change agent may be anywhere in the organisation and will meet with denial from above and below. If the change agent is a 'change generator', either as 'key change agent' or a 'demonstrator', he or she will need the support of 'patrons' and 'defenders' to enforce the drive for change.

Resistance to change comprises cognitive and emotional elements which arise from the context of the change or the individual's inability to deal with change. The starting place for dealing with resistance is to consider it as a healthy, self-regulating manifestation which must be respected and taken seriously by superiors and consultants. Denial must be treated in this manner. On the cognitive dimension, the substantive issues of why change is needed, the degree of choice which exists about whether to change or not, the nature and strength of the forces driving change, the effect of the change on individuals and teams, must be presented in such a manner that the individual can assess the perceived impact of the change in the light of as full information about the change as is possible. On the emotional dimension, listening to fears, empathetically understanding different perspectives on the change, and creating the facilitative climate whereby individuals can be enabled to acknowledge and come to terms with personal emotional forces inhibiting participation in change, is a necessary process for superiors and consultants. In short, for movement to occur there has to be sufficient psychological safety whereby the change data can be accepted as valid, relevant and pertinent. In other words, some unfreezing has begun to take place.

At the same time, the acknowledgement of the need for change is somewhat generic. The acknowledgement that change is required is not necessarily internalised immediately. A reluctant acknowledgement shifts the impetus for change to other parts of the system. When this happens the change has shifted to a dodging stage. It must be acknowledged that some may remain in the denial mode and continue to persist in denying that change is needed. For such, the change process may move on without them, and at a later stage they have to reassess their position.

A province of a order, in its efforts to initiate planned change arising from Vatican II, conducted a survey of needs of the country in
which it ministered. The results of the survey were presented to
several meetings of the senior members, in conjunction with
research on the current and projected future state of existing ministries and personnel, and the necessity of transformational change
was outlined. The need for transformational change was denied
and countered with the scenario that things would fundamentally
continue as they had done.

The provincial of the time set about establishing a renewal programme to enable the system to unfreeze by focusing on individual
development to meet the emotional issues and by setting up
numerous task forces and commissions around specific policy areas
to deal with the substantive change issues. Over the following several years, the agenda for change became established throughout
the province and its members. However, many members continued
to resist and refused to participate. While they might acknowledge
the need for change in a general, theoretical way, they chose to
remain outside the mainstream of developments. They in effect
opted out, continued in their own mindset and resented any
attempts by superiors to change them. They continued their opposition, either by not attending meetings or by remaining silent at
them and by complaining and voicing opposition at informal gath-
erings and among their peers. In subsequent years, as the change
momentum became more established and as change took place, this
group decreased in number, as some gradually began to participate
in the changed province and others retired. Some chose to remain
outside the mainstream of a changed province.

Second Stage: Dodging

The above example illustrates the essential difference between the
denying and the dodging stages within unfreezing. The dodging
stage begins when the accumulated evidence shows that the change
is likely to take place. It is acknowledged reluctantly that some
change is needed, but that the change is required in other parts of
the system – 'Others have to change'. There can be a searching for
countervailing data, which allow the individual or team or community to avoid or postpone having to change.

Because the push for change is coming from outside, i.e. the provincial, anger is expressed typically in a passive-aggressive non-participation. The anger is directed towards the change agents, with a more specific direction than the anger which might occur at the denial stage. At the dodging stage the anger is directed at 'those who are making me change'. Effort is devoted to diverting the change or at least finding some way to be peripheral to it. The energy for this comes from many sources. Frustration, lack of ownership, fear of change, are some possible sources. To return to the example of the introduction of a province plan, it can be expressed as: 'It is only the fad of the current provincial. The next provincial will probably have a different focus, so we don't have to take this too seriously.'

At the same time, this can be a creative stage. This stage has its active components though it is characterised by hedging and not getting involved. An individual can confuse the issue by presenting the weakness of the approach to the change. There may be a more serious issue that needs to be dealt with first. This shifts the action to a different focus. Another method to subvert is to change the form. If the discussion is on apostolic priorities, change it to personnel. If it is on personnel, change it to continuing formation. The mode of agreement is often silence, which can be, and is often, misread as opposition. Movement comes when sufficient ownership of the need for the change is accepted.

The generic approaches to dealing with resistance, outlined in the denying section, above are also applicable to the dodging stage. The issues on the cognitive and emotional dimensions must be dealt with through a process of consultation, listening and serious consideration of the concerns expressed. Movement out of the dodging stage comes either when, out of the consultation process, ownership of the need for change is accepted and the changing process can begin, or after some time has elapsed, when others have been implementing the change and the implications and effects of the change are perceived differently and perhaps appreciated, or at least perceived less negatively. In terms of the Lewin-Schein model, the elements of disconfirmation, the presence of sufficient guilt or anxiety, and the creation of psychological safety, are present so unfreezing has occurred.

Third Stage: Doing

The doing stage is where the need for change has been acknowledged and owned to the degree that explorations of what changes are required, how, where, at what cost and at what cost to whom, are undertaken. The doing stage is not comprised of any one action; it is a whole series of actions – diagnosing the forces driving and restraining change, interpreting data, articulating a desired future, having intermediate stages, creating and following a change plan, generating commitment, managing the transition, negotiating and bargaining, implementing, reviewing, and so on (which will be discussed in chapter 5). It may be spread over a considerable time. The focus moves from the 'change generators' to the 'change implementors'. As the change process unfolds, issues of where change must occur in the present system, how that change should be made, and what cost, must be diagnosed, decided upon and implemented. The change process, whether utilising a scanning, role identification or a combination of both, tests the readiness and capability of the system to change.

Within a province, the change process necessitates dealing with controversy and disagreement regarding different diagnoses and proposed solutions and dealing with the conflict which inevitably arises in such a context. Conflict at the doing stage is more focused than at the denial and dodging stages, as it occurs within the context of a change plan, and in this regard is different from conflict at the dodging stage. The issue is not whether change is required, but what change is required in what parts of the system and affecting what apostolates and communities. Indeed, on particular issues regarding possible solutions to a change problem, there may be a reversal to denial and dodging. The members of a particular apostolate may have bought into the change plan but, when they see that it is their apostolate that is to be phased out, they may revert to denial and dodging. So each proposal may initiate its own change stages, so that within the broader change process, a particular proposal may generate denial and dodging and require to be dealt with in those terms.

As the specific change is worked on, more things are uncovered that require change. Minor moves, such as budgeting, restructuring, allocation of personnel, continuing formation, emerge. These may have to be worked on so as to facilitate the major change. For the superior, the general tendency is to let the momentum take over. The difficult part of gaining consent and involvement is over, so sit back and let it happen. This is dangerous for two reasons. It is important to ensure that the change endeavour does not negatively affect relationships between various teams or between apostolic units. Polarisations between groups of individuals, i.e. young and old, school ministry versus health care ministry, may emerge from the process of the change, which will require active facilitation and management by superiors. Secondly, there is the danger of over-loading the change process with trying too many things in addition to the ones that began the change process. The organisation has the capability and the readiness to change. The tendency is to overload. There needs to be discernment as to what can or cannot be put into the change. As one provincial put it, 'We cannot add in yet another call to conversion'.

Fourth Stage: Sustaining

As normative behaviour is difficult to change, some reinforcement of changed habits is necessary to ensure that change survives and the change state is sustained. This is the refreezing stage and the 'change adopters' come into promi-nence. The successful completion of this stage is the integration of the change into the habitual patterns of behaviour and structure.

> *As normative change is difficult to sustain, some reinforcement is necessary to ensure that change survives.*

For the individual, the new state must be reinforced by how the change fits the individual, the team and community, the province and is congruent with the order's charism. This systemic reinforce-ment constitutes the psychological basis of rewarding the continu-ance of the change state. For the individual members of a religious order, key changes are sustained through internalising a new understanding of what it means to be a minister in the church in the latter part of the twentieth century, in the light of a developing theology and spirituality of ministry, which is finding some expres-sion in the organisational changes which are taking place.

In organisational terms, this stage is best defined as the implement-ation of operating procedures and is a key stage of any change

process. It is the focusing of energy to follow through on programmes and projects. Sometimes new manners of proceeding,
new information systems or even new endeavours, mark this stage.
At this point, the order needs to be attuned to the fact that change is
part of life. It will have in place the ability to sense changes in the
environment and to adapt quickly to them. In this respect, sustaining or refreezing does not attempt to create a new stability or close
down future change, but maintain an openness to continuous
forces for change. Apostolic review is the key process to sustain the
change. This is a process whereby religious teams, apostolates and
provinces reflect on plans and their implementation in a discerning
manner as a sort of corporate apostolic examen.

TRANSFORMATIONAL CHANGE

At this point it is necessary to point to the fact that there are several
different degrees of change. Some changes involve solving a particular problem. A problem is named, its causes identified, solutions
are generated, selected and implemented without any alteration to
the structure of the situation. A provincial needs to replace a superior
whose term of office is completed. So there is consultation, a short
list drawn up and eventually a successor appointed. A change has
taken place and the system remains as it is. This sort of change is
typically referred to as first-order change or incremental change.

A more complex change occurs when there is lateral thinking and
the core assumptions which underlie a situation are questioned and
altered. This can occur when first-order solutions don't work and
there is a realisation that new thinking is required. This is referred
to as second-order or transformational change. Religious life itself
is undergoing such a transformational change. The old concepts do
not fit any more; the new wine cannot be put into old wineskins.
What is required now is a complete redefinition of religious life and
ministry and a formulation of new assumptions. Of course the danger with second-order change is that once it is implemented it
becomes institutionalised and reinforced by first-order solutions.

Third-order change occurs when members of an organisation learn
to question their own assumptions and points of view and develop
and implement new ones. Third-order change is in the realm of
conversion and of the collective development of a spirituality of

apostolic review and renewal. In third-order change, the habit of
questioning assumptions and renewal is normative.

It is important to acknowledge these different degrees of change.
Clearly, third-order change is much more complex and difficult
than an incremental alteration within the existing system. One les-
son from such an acknowledgement is that when incremental solu-

*The future of religious life lies
in third-order change*

tions do not seem to be having their
desired effect, a redefinition of the
situation and addressing the prob-
lem from a different perspective may be required. Ultimately, the
future of religious life lies in the domain of third-order change.

CONCLUSIONS

In this chapter a generic change model which states that any change
process is comprised of three stages – recognising and owning that
change is needed, making the appropriate change and then making
the change survive and work – was introduced. There are issues
within each stage which have to be acknowledged and managed.
Recognising that change is needed may be painful and so a great
deal of support may be necessary to help an individual or group to
come to terms with a need for change. We can expect people to feel
angry, confused, hurt or excited. Knowing what to change, and
managing how to do it, is a separate set of issues and skills.
Sustaining a change so that a system does not slip back into old
habits requires yet another set of activities. In the following chapters, the change process will be applied to the organisational setting
of a religious order and some of the complexities explored.

CHAPTER 5

Managing Apostolic Change

The renewal of complex systems such as apostolic ministries is essentially about who is going to do what, in what parts of the system, in order to move the system from an existing state, with which there is some dissatisfaction, to a renewed state. There are three situations or states of being with regard to a change endeavour. There is the present state, with which there is some dissatisfaction or desire to change. There is the future state, which is the desired outcome of the change process. There is the transition state, which is the period between the present and the future states and where the change process takes place.

THE ADAPTIVE COPING CYCLE OF ORGANISATIONS

The process whereby information is received into an organisation, processed and transformed into output, is a cycle of continuous coping and adaptation (Figure 5-1). This cycle has five steps, beginning with a change in some aspects of the organisation's external or internal environment, and ending with a more adaptive, renewed organisation. While these steps are separated conceptually, in practice they overlap and occur concurrently as an organisation is in constant interaction with its environment. In an organisation development programme, the five steps of the adaptive coping cycle provide a framework for managing the change process in a complex system, such as a religious order, a province or a ministry province, and for those working in a consultative role with superiors.

1. Sensing a change in some part of the internal or external environment.

2. Importing the relevant information about the change into those parts of the province that can act upon it, and digesting the implications of that information.

3. Making changes in the province – changing apostolates or

making changes in apostolates – according to the information obtained, while managing the implications of those changes in other aspects of the province's life, and stabilising the change.

4. Exporting a new service to the people the province serves, which is more in line with the originally perceived changes in the environment.

5. Obtaining feedback on the success of the change through further sensing of the state of the external environment and the degree of integration within the province. The movement through the six steps involves sensitivity to process – how vision is articulated, how commitment is built, where interventions are judged to be necessary or desired – so that the change is made effectively.

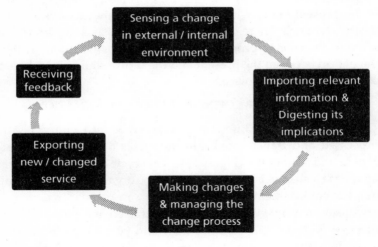

Figure 5-1
The Adaptive Coping Cycle

Any organisation can have dysfunctions on any of these five steps. It can fail to sense changes in the environment or it can misinterpret them. It can fail to transmit the relevant information to those parts of the system which can act upon it. The information may fail to have the impact of creating change. A change may not result in a renewed output or there may be inadequate feedback of the effect of the changed service on the client which enables the organisation to reassess its strategic role and function. Each of the steps requires specific attention in order that the organisation adapt successfully to a changing environment.

1. Sensing a Change in Some Part of the Internal or External Environment

'Why change?' is a good opening question. This is the first step of the adaptive coping cycle whereby disconfirming information is identified and change is put on the agenda. The identification of the forces driving change is critical as, in the long run, whatever changes are made must provide an adequate response to these forces. The forces for change may be coming from the external environment, such as the call to new renewed mission, developing social needs, or from having to adapt to changing government policy. The forces for change may also come from within the order, such as the need for new ministries, for restructuring a ministry, the need to divest large properties, to adapt the balance of ministries in a province in the light of ageing personnel, the renewal of formation processes, to take a few examples. Given the identification of forces for change the question to be asked is, 'What needs changing?' The potency of forces is weighted and major change forces are distinguished from the minor ones.

'Why change?' is a good opening question.

A second key element in evaluating the need for change is the degree of choice about whether to change or not. This is often an overlooked question. In some instances, there is no control over the forces demanding change. In other instances, there is a great deal of control over the change. In that case, there is likely to be a good deal of scope as to what changes, how, and in what timescale the change can take place.

The process of taking in disconfirming information, assessing it and acting on it, constitutes the initial core elements of a change process. The traditional term for this stage is unfreezing, i.e. that which has been solid is now unfrozen so that it can be manipulated to meet the demands of change. Because disconfirming information demands change of some form, it is frequently threatening and can create anxiety. Accordingly, a very natural reaction to the demand for change is to resist until the situation is assessed and understood. Therefore, it is useful, at this juncture, to examine how individuals deal with change in the organisations in which they work.

Some people find change difficult because of elements of their own personality. For instance, they may be set in their ways and find it extremely difficult to change their ways of working or thinking. They may have created a strong identity between who they are and what they do, so any change in what they do becomes personal. Undoubtedly, some individuals are afflicted with psychological neuroses. Yet to reduce resistance to change to personality, and locate the blame only on the individual, does not do justice to either the individual or to the complexity of an organisational change process. Those resisting change may be some of the most intelligent and high-powered members of the order. Resistance to change is also situational, that is that the way the situation is managed may itself create the resistance. Resistance may be grounded in how people have been treated by previous superiors.

When leaders initiate changes which affect the lives of others, there are three critical elements in how people respond. First, there is the perception of the changes. This comprises what the changes mean, the degree of control the individual has over them, and the degree of trust the individual has in the persons initiating the change. Second, the individual assesses the impact the change will have. Will it be destructive, threatening, probably negative, probably positive, enhancing...? Thirdly, how will the individual respond – oppose, resist, tolerate, accept, support or embrace the change? These three elements are heavily influenced by the availability of information about the change and the process of communication between those promoting the change and those affected by it. Absence of information and a lack of a sense of psychological participation creates uncertainty, hesitation and resistance, and increases any lack of trust which might exist. If an organisation's leadership does not reduce the anxiety which paralyses change, by creating sufficient psychological safety, then resistance to learning and change will become more entrenched. The importance of an individual's spirituality must not be underestimated. An individual's struggle with change, when brought to prayer, may uncover a deep sense of unworthiness, inadequacy before God or sinfulness. The process of becoming free to change is not automatic or guaranteed; it is a complex spiritual psychological journey. Ultimately it is a gift.

Resistance has both cognitive and affective elements. It is not only about anger, frustration, enthusiasm or excitement. An individual may resist a change because he or she does not think it will solve the particular problem and has an alternative solution. In this instance, resistance is grounded in a different assessment of what the problems are and how they might be resolved. Dealing with resistance involves not only listening empathically to those who feel hurt by the change, but also re-evaluating the analysis of the problems and the proposed courses of action. Such an approach to meeting resistance attempts to harness the dynamic energy which is currently being channelled into resistance.

2. Importing the Relevant Information about the Change into those Parts of the Order that can Act on it and Digesting the Implications of that Information

The second step of the adaptive coping cycle is that of taking the disconfirming information into the apostolic teams of the order or province and reflecting on its application and implications. Once a sense of the need for change has been established, the most useful focus for attention is to define a future state. This process is essentially that of having a wide-angled view of the future in the form of a detailed picture of what the province or apostolate would look like after change has taken place. A specific time should be defined. Many of the approaches used by consultants that focus on future-scenario writing, ideal future, future stakeholder demands, worst-case scenario, can be utilised. One approach I frequently use with provincials is to ask them to portray the province as they would like it to be when they hand over to their successor in six or so years time. That provides a concrete and manageable timeframe for an individual provincial to formulate a vision towards which he can work. What is essential is that the future be portrayed in terms of charism and mission (typically through criteria), have some analytic judgement as to what the environment of the future will be, and thirdly, be different from a future that is simply a linear extension of the present without any intervention.

> *Once the need for change has been established, the most useful focus for attention is to define a future state.*

The process of defining the future is a function of the top levels of leadership. It provides a focus for leadership attention and facilitates insight into the more specific strategic details. For the change process to be successful, it must be owned and led from the top. This is not to say that the process should be top-down, but simply to affirm the core role of leadership in owning the change process. In a religious order, it is typically the major superior and council who ultimately mission the individual, even though the initiative and investigation of options has been done by the individual. The process of defining the future state at the outset is critical as it helps animate motivation and energy because it describes the future in a positive light. On the other hand, an initial focus on the imperfect present may over-emphasise negative experiences and generate pessimism. The description of the future can provide those not involved in defining the future state with a picture of how they might fit into the future. This can be a way of dealing with resistance by reducing anxiety and uncertainty.

The 'Why change?' question and the desired future must be communicated through the province in a manner that facilitates understanding of why change is needed, what the possible alternatives are, and enabling ideas and solutions to surface, be discussed, discerned and confirmed.

Up to this point the actual need for change has only been implied. The need for change must be made explicit in the light of an accurate description of the present and of the defined desired future. The key process in this review is a clear and accurate picture of the present and a diagnosis of the current reality – what the order's/apostolate's current strengths and weaknesses are. This snapshot of the present points to the significant question, 'What needs changing for the planned change to be effective?' Because the present is assessed in the light of the desired future, a judgement can be made as to what needs changing and what does not. For the change to effectively take place, a change in current structures, attitudes, policies or activities may be needed. Some of the present ways of doing things might require changing. As any change problem is a cluster of possible changes, particular problems may be grouped under common headings, i.e. community life. The problem is then described more specifically. The subsequent questions to be answered are, 'Which of these requires priority attention? If A is changed will a solution to B fall more easily into place? What needs to be done first?'

A second element in describing the present is to describe the relevant parts of the province that will be involved in the change. This description points to the critical mass of people needed for the change to take place. Examples might include the superiors, those involved in teaching ministry, and those in formation. Their readiness and capability for change must be assessed. Readiness points to the motivation and willingness to change, while capability refers to whether they are able, psychologically and otherwise, to change. Ways of increasing readiness and capability may be planned and implemented. In one province, the provincial used a strategy of focusing on the individual through the promotion of sensitivity training. The overall effect of the sensitivity training on the province was the beginnings of a gradual change of culture. Participants in the groups learned to become more open to change in themselves and to listen to others in their change.

Resistance may continue at this stage as individuals and teams assess the impact of the change on them and on their work in the province. The provincial and consultants continue to listen to the issues, respond to them, negotiate appropriate and suitable outcomes and adjust the change plan where necessary to accommodate changes arising out of discernment and continuing interaction with members of the province.

3. Making Changes in the Province – Changing Apostolates or Making Changes within Apostolates – according to the information obtained while managing the implications of those changes for other aspects of the province's life, and stabilising the change

This step is what is generally perceived as being the actual change process though, as we have seen, preparation for change is equally essential to the process. The critical task is to move from the present to the future and manage the intervening period of transition. The primary task is to move from the present to the future by assessing the present in terms of the future so as to determine what needs to be done.

> *The critical task is to move from the present to the future and manage the intervening period of transition.*

This transition state between the present and the future is typically a difficult time because the past is found to be deficient and no longer tenable and the new state has not yet come into being. So, in essence, the transition state is a somewhat unique state and so needs to be managed as such. The uniqueness of the transition state is that it can be characterised by uncertainty, stress, levels of energy which are often undirected or negatively directed. The past is idealised. There are demands for clear leadership and there may be intergroup conflict, particularly as some will be seen to benefit from the change while others will not. There are demands on the leadership to cope positively with these issues. Energy, especially negative energy, needs to be redirected and managed. There is a high demand on communication of information. The concern that the apostolate is suffering during the change must be met and the leadership must be trusted, respected and perceived as competent. Leadership, to manage these conditions, must psychologically accept uncertainty as essential to the situation. The future goals must be clearly and explicitly defined with intermediate goals and plans plotted. As already emphasised, the commitment and confidence of leadership to the change and the future must be assured. In short, this transition state must be consciously managed because it is a unique state.

There are two aspects to managing this transition state. One is to identify the relevant tasks and activities to be undertaken. A change plan is devised. A change plan is simply the identification of the forms the strategic plan takes – goals, activities, structures, projects and experiments that will help achieve the desired state. It must be purposeful, task-specific, integrated into the general purpose, be defined in temporal terms, be adaptable, and have a solid measure of support behind it. The choice of where to begin offers the following options. The change can begin at the top, where provincials model and implement the change themselves. Another approach is to begin in those areas where there is already a readiness to change, or the areas where there is the most hurt or pain for which the change will be a remedy. A new apostolate or community can be an experiment of the change; a temporary community can be set up to try it out. The choice of intervention for managing the change should be a decision made later rather than earlier in the process. It is the end than creates the means. In others, leadership should think out where they are going and where they want to get to before starting to do something. Structures such as experiments, continuing formation interventions, temporary structures, networks of meetings to discuss the present, might be utilised. Many provinces have used special community meetings, province assemblies, renewal courses, experimental communities and task-forces.

 The second aspect of transition management is to set up the structures and mechanisms necessary to accomplish those tasks. There are different ways of structuring this management. The provincial can personally take charge of the change project or appoint an individual who would have the necessary status to manage it. It can be managed by a task-force or committee, such as a ministries commission. This can be formed through the formal hierarchy of the province, i.e. through the superiors, or by having representatives from different constituencies, or by bringing together the natural informal leaders. In recent years it has not been uncommon to find someone on the provincial team or council with the assigned role of co-ordinator of planning.

No amount of change can take place without commitment. The planners of the change must take into account those whose commitment is needed for the change to take place, and evolve a commitment plan to build that commitment. The commitment plan focuses on who in the province or apostolate must be committed to the change if it is to take place. There may be partic-

> *No amount of change can take place without commitment.*

ular individuals whose support is a prerequisite for the change, and a critical mass whose commitment is necessary to provide the energy and support for the change to occur. One way by which commitment to the change can be worked at is by involving members of the province through particular events, such as province assemblies, membership of task-forces, continuing formation courses, and so on. Such processes do not guarantee success and, in the final count, there will be those who feel out of the renewal and choose to remain outside of any plan.

If a plan to create commitment to the change is not well managed or is unsuccessful, then individual religious may find themselves in a pattern of demotivation and alienation from the order. Some individuals may opt to leave the order. For others, leaving may not be a viable option, so disillusioned religious may opt to drift into a mindset of persistent grumbling where they complain and grumble about conditions and how things are. Some individuals manage to find a niche for themselves in which they create their own private enclave and reduce interdependence with others.

Defensive behaviour is described in terms of individuals avoiding action by over-conforming, passing the buck, playing dumb, depersonalising and stalling and avoiding blame by playing safe, justifying and scapegoating. The final option is to collaborate with others who feel the same as they do in creating a collective delusion which becomes a neurotic mechanism. So there is blaming, hostility, aggression, anger, feelings of frustration, and dysfunctional organisational behaviour. Collective neurotic behaviour in an organisation results in individuals feeling frustrated and alienated and so they seek refuge in informal mechanisms by being apathetic and disinterested towards the contemporary order and manifesting defensive reactions such as day dreaming, aggression, ambivalence, projection and regression. Informal groups to sanction these defensive reactions are created and so ministry and community life are retarded. This behaviour has a cumulative effect, feeds back into the province and reinforces itself. In such a scenario, the intended planned organisational change may be severely retarded and may generate the need for further interventions. As I have already indicated, there are frequently reasons for this state of mind in the individuals' history in the order – how they were treated in their formation or at a later stage by previous provincials and superiors.

The late 1980s and the 1990s constitute a good example of a transition state for religious orders. Many traditional ministries cannot be carried on as they have been in the past, yet how to divest them or hand them over is not clear and takes time. It is clear that religious orders will be smaller in size in fifteen to twenty years time, while at the moment there is an increasing number of ageing religious who must be cared for at the present and so there is need for institutional communities which can provide such care on such a scale. Provincials are currently attempting to manage this transition by fostering the apostolic energy of the younger and more active members towards the ministries of the future, while at the same time managing the maintenance of existing ministries and caring for the elderly. For provincials, such situations pose enormous dilemmas. As architects of purpose, they have a responsibility to strategically lead the province into the future, and so collective defensive behaviour is perceived as barriers to renewal and change. As personal leaders, they love and care for all the members of their province as fellow religious. Such dilemmas are not easily resolved. Ultimately, provincials must help their provinces to be renewed and care for those who feel alienated or unable to change.

4. *Exporting new services to the people the order serves, which are in line with the originally perceived changes in the environment*

The change process must impact the actual apostolic activity of the order. The outcome of the change process may be new apostolates, apostolates exercised in a new or different way, community life which enables ministry to be exercised in a new or different way, and so on. The change efforts must be directly related to (a) the actual mission of the order, and (b) the forces pushing for change. So new or different ministries which emerge from the change process must relate to what the original disconfirmation of experience pointed to and be congruent with the mission of the order.

5. *Obtaining feedback on the success of the change through further sensing of the state of the external environment and the degree of integration within the province*

Once the change is in place, it must be stabilised and maintained. There is an awkward balance or tension in institutionalising change while maintaining an openness to further change. Provincials and superiors must attend to the notion of continuous transition by building in review processes. This can be done through periodic but regular review meetings by specific teams, renewal assemblies and perhaps periodic visits from some external reviewer – the provincial in the case of an apostolate, perhaps the consultant who helped facilitate the change.

Evaluation is the process of gathering and analysing information, undertaken to provide those responsible for the leadership of the change with a satisfactory progress of the effects and/or progress of the change effort. Evaluation must be planned with clear purposes. Evaluation can be an intervention that reviews outcomes and refocuses energy and commitment. What needs to be determined is what is required so as to avoid overload, and to link evaluation with reward. Reward for the religious is a complex spiritual and psychological process. At its depth, it is an affirmation that one's ministry is in tune with the mission and vocation of the order. It may also involve a concrete reward to an apostolate from a major superior, i.e. further allocation of scarce resources, such as money or personnel.

As emphasised earlier, the focus of review is learning from experience. What has the province, as a collective system, learned from the experience of the change process? Individuals may be learning, but that is not a guarantee that the system learns. Religious orders, as any organisation, may go through cycles of decisions and consequences which individuals easily recognise as repeating mistakes.

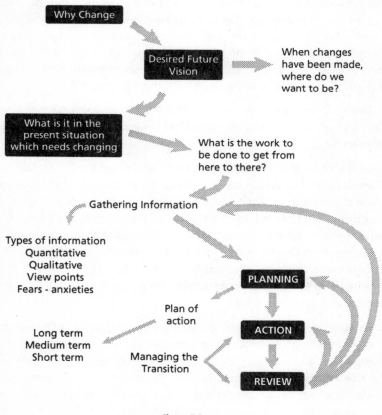

Figure 5-2
Elements of the Change Process

Yet the system frequently does not seem to have that same recognition.

Evaluation cannot only be an internal activity, where members and close associates participate in a review process. Evaluation must involve feedback from those to whom the order ministers. Not to include such a constituency returns the religious order into a closed system and closes it off from the very insertion and apostolic activity it may be espousing. If the people whom the change process was aimed to help do not perceive it as such, then review is critical.

CONCLUSIONS

Change, especially organisational change, is a complex process (Figure 5-2). A change effort requires understanding, especially by leadership, of the complexities of intervention. It requires attention to many different tasks. This chapter has laid out a series of processes for an organisational change effort. It has emphasised the importance of defining the future before assessing the present. It has focused on the need to plan how the change will be managed in its transition stage and how commitment can be strengthened. It stresses the essential need to have people and structures working in harmony. It provides a conceptual map for planning the steps of the change process.

Phases and Levels of Apostolic Renewal

In chapter 4 a generic model of change was presented, comprising three stages of unfreezing, changing and refreezing, and described four psychological reactions to change. These reactions occur as the change process is initiated and develops within an order. As the change process moves through a complex system, such as a religious order, there is a chronological process as the 'change generators' get the change agenda into the formal system and the major superior as 'implementor' begins an exploration and implementation of the change. The provincial typically takes the change issue to the council, and through the council to the province, and so on until the change affects the entire system, both internally and externally. The unfreezing, changing and refreezing in a complex system involves individuals, teams and communities, hearing the news of the proposed change, reacting to it and deciding how to respond. What is required is that there is a critical mass whose support is needed for movement to occur and change to take place.

In chapter 5 the core processes to manage change through the adaptive coping cycle were outlined. Recognising the need for change, articulating a desired future, describing the present to see what requires changing, developing commitment and managing the transition, were some of the key processes identified in moving a change through a system. These steps detail how the reactions to change interact with the four levels. There are very many activities and interactions in a large system's change process, but I have grouped many of them together to form a seven phase sequence in order that the process may not seem too cumbersome (Table 6-1). The phases attempt to map how the change process moves through an organisation – across the four levels, taking account of how individuals, teams and communities, the province and the order moves through the denial, dodging, doing and sustaining stages.

Phase 1 DISCONFIRMATION	
Key individual	Denying, Dodging
Phase 2 INITIATION	
Key individual	Doing
Council members	Denying, Dodging
Phase 3 MANOEUVRING	
Key individual	Doing
Council members	Doing
Province members	Denying, Dodging
Phase 4 INTEGRATION	
Key individual	Doing
Council members	Doing
Province members	Doing
Order	Denying, Dodging
Phase 5 ACTION	
Key individual	Sustaining
Council members	Doing
Province members	Doing
Order	Doing
Phase 6 FOLLOW-THROUGH	
Key individual	Sustaining
Council members	Sustaining
Province members	Doing
Order	Doing
Phase 7 SUSTAINING	
All	Sustaining

Table 6-1
Phases and Levels of Apostolic Change

PHASE 1: DISCONFIRMATION
The Key Individual Denying and Dodging

Change enters the order through an individual. That individual as a 'generator' goes through his/her own reaction to the need for change by initially denying the validity, relevance and pertinence of the change. Once that is recognised, that the change does apply, it can be dodged and applied to others – 'I don't have to do anything. I can leave it to others. Only minor adjustments are required.' This gives way to a realisation that the information is real and pertinent, perhaps that the province's ministry is in peril if something isn't done.

If the individuals in question are not in a formal, hierarchical position or role, they may have to approach someone that is, in order that the change issue be placed on the agenda. They may approach superiors, directors of apostolates, council members and present the issue. The persons approached will go through their own stages of denying and dodging till they accept the issue as pertinent and relevant and move to the doing stage. In some instances this process is repeated until it reaches the key individual, possibly the provincial, who has the power to generate movement on the change. When this individual acts and is prepared to articulate the need for change to others, then this phase is concluded.

One provincial, prior to taking up office, attended some meetings and courses which transformed his thinking about the need for change in his province and role of the leader must take. He learned that change had to be led from the top so he became determined to use his leadership role in creating change. At this stage, he had unfrozen and was prepared to lead change in a directive manner.

PHASE 2: INITIATION
The Key Individual Doing and the Team Denying and Dodging

When key individuals have worked through the psychological reactions of denial and dodging the change, they move to the doing stage and present the change data to their ministry team, emphasising the necessity for change and beginning to define the dimensions of the change. This could be a provincial presenting a change issue to a council. The individual members of the council themselves go through the denial and dodging stages, and so the council as a team does also. The team denies – this is not relevant. Then it dodges – we don't have to do anything about it now – and enters into a period of vocal bargaining. The tendency to criticise the one who has brought the bad news must be recognised. This phase is concluded when the council, as team, recognises the issue as critical and acknowledges the need to do something. Ownership of an articulated problem ends this phase, not just as defined by an individual, but as articulated by the team through consensus. There will be individuals who do not support the change but are not powerful enough to block or stop it.

To return to the earlier example, the provincial, on assuming office, was determined to generate change in the province. There were two commissions, set up by his predecessor, which were concluding their work. One had been conducting a survey of the needs in the country and the other had been reviewing the order's existing ministries and the present and future state of personnel resources. The provincial decided to use the occasion of the completion of the two commissions' work as the entry point for change. He persuaded his consultors that the work of the two committees was the catalyst of initiating change.

PHASE 3: MANOEUVRING
The Key Individual and Team Doing and the Province Denying and Dodging

This phase involves bringing multiple ministry teams and communities at the province level to address the change issue. The province, in its members, denies the validity, relevance and pertinence of the change. Cultural assumptions are central as history and tradition are used to block change. Each team or community tends to view the change issue from its own viewpoint and may deny the validity, relevance and pertinence of the change. It will be evident in the province that some apostolates will have to diminish and some will have to grow, that some apostolates are more critical than others, that some activities will be let go and others developed.

Denial at the province level typically means the emergence of differing and conflicting interpretations of the data supporting the change. The information driving the change is not accurate, reliable and is open to differing interpretations. The political inter-relationship between teams may be a factor in denial, as for instance, when the need for change is denied by one team because the change is being promoted by a specific other team. The culture of sub-cultures within the organisation is used, as history and tradition are used, to block change.

The process of dodging needs to be addressed by strategic management. The interfacing of different ministries – common education policy, common policy for health-care ministries, continuing formation – in terms of allocation of personnel and other resources are the most relevant ones for areas of difficulty. The critical aspect of evaluating the need for change and getting ownership is to see the problem in a new way. The dodging stage at this level confronts the assumption that the province is made up of independent ministries. Each ministry team must be conscious of what others do and how, and how what they do interacts with what others do. Creation and ownership of a sense of province is essential. This phase ends with agreement on the articulation of the problem and the process steps needed to introduce change. Typically this involves correct identification of the critical people needed to make the change at a province level, and description of what the future state of the province would look like. The phase concludes with ownership of the question of what effect the change will have on the order's relationship with the external environment.

There is a complex reality behind any statement that asserts that a province is at the doing stage of change. While the denying and dodging stages are repeated by every individual, many do not proceed to the doing stage. For the change to move on a province level a critical mass of members is required ('adopters'). Those that do not accept the change and who are not powerful enough to block it can become peripheral to or alienated from the system. Some move to the doing stage long after the change has been implemented and established.

There is a danger of regression, particularly at Phases 2 and 3. As the key individual experiences the team's denial, and as the team experiences the province's denial, it is often noticed that the individual or the team can lose confidence and slip back into a dodging mode. A provincial may feel very hurt by the rejection of the council or the province and withdraw into a dodging mode – 'I did my best. As they don't want to face the issues it is up to my successor to deal with it'. The presence of a consultant can be significant in confronting this tendency and in helping the superior and the team process what is going on and remain firm in their convictions.

Following on the earlier example, the provincial presented the findings of two commissions (one which had surveyed environmental needs and the other which had reviewed existing ministries and personnel) to a representative meeting of the province's senior members. His approach was to emphasise the changing nature of the environment (as expressed in the needs survey) and to support his argument with the data on the region's limited resources and declining personnel. He invited participation in decision-making about the future and the comprehensive change which, in his view, faced the order. In organisational levels terms, he attempted strategic change on Level IV to a Level III representative gathering. The response was largely one of denial. The participants at the meeting denied the need for fundamental change, defended their own constituencies from the threat of such change, asserted that what had been done before could continue, and effectively blocked the provincial's efforts at involving them.

The provincial felt isolated and wanted to resign. The superior-general gave him unqualified support to continue. The provincial analysed the situation and decided to initiate a large personal development and spirituality programme, through which many members participated in sensitivity training, directed retreats and spirituality workshops, in order to promote the individual and enable individuals to grow in self-awareness (a Level I directed intervention).

At the same time, an OD consultant was hired to gather the members' feedback on how they saw the province. After a frank report was published, the provincial, with the consultant's help, established an internal consultancy team to help bring about change. A number of task forces were set up with members of the province serving on them, and the consultancy team provided a service by doing research and facilitating meetings. During the three years of this work, there was a gradual movement towards recognising that change was inevitable (movement from denial), though many attempted to opt out and others left it to the provincial to keep the pressure on (dodging).

That particular provincial completed his term of office. His successor initiated team-building workshops and mandated ministry teams and communities to hold meetings on particular topics with external consultants present. Over a two year period, he attempted to facilitate the development of team skills (Level II) as a natural follow-on to the sensitivity training and to integrate the content of the change issues into the process. He emphasised co-responsibility and participation in the process of change. Over his six years, the threat that change posed appeared to lessen. The change agenda was now established and was integrated into the ongoing process of the province.

PHASE 4: INTEGRATION

The Key Individual, Team and Province Doing, the Order Denying and Dodging

Initially in this phase, the question is about how the order and its stakeholders perceive themselves and the order, if the change is introduced. For example, if the order moves to be more closely identified with the poor, what the reaction of the current clientele of the order's schools would be is asked. At first the change is denied and when that is accepted, the question of what the least amount of change is acceptable is asked. Successful change requires an understanding of stakeholder demands and behaviour and a proactive stance taken in their regard.

In the example we are following in this chapter, the provincial, the third in this sequence, went about articulating a strategic plan. He openly declared his intention, set up groups across the region to draft policy statements on the main areas, articulated and emphasised the particular process to be followed, and actively led the process himself. It was an active 'doing' stage on Level III as the province was confronted with policies and decisions touching each sector of the province's ministries. The outcome was an integrated strategic plan which articulated the order's mission, the environmental needs, the order's resources, the decisions and the action steps (Level IV). At this juncture the change was still in the internal province level at Level III. The order had not yet brought the change to its stakeholders, which had its traditional expectations of what and how the order conducted its ministries.

PHASE 5: ACTION
The Key Individual Sustaining, The Team, Province and Order Doing

The key individual goes into a sustaining stage, when energy is no longer required to initiate the change effort. The energy of the key individual is released to look for ways of sustaining the change. This may involve working with the consultant as to what structures may be required to keep the change in place and seeing how others have done it. The focus at this point is on the process of restructuring, rather than the content of the change. This phase is concluded when the key individuals have enabled the team to own the sustaining issues, and they can look at other data and other change issues.

Phase 5 is the critical phase in which, for the first time, some question surfaces of whether or not first- or second-order change is required. The adequacy or inadequacy of the change as perceived and implemented is reviewed in the context of its effects on the long-term perspective of the organisation and its ability to engage in continuous change.

Continuing the example, the change process moved to a situation where the strategic plan, which had been introduced, was being implemented at local level and was having on impact on the order's relationship with its stakeholders. For example, in relation to one of the order's high schools, there was some re-assessment by staff, parents and alumni as to the changed state regarding what the order's new understanding of its mission involved, and a new relationship with the school and its values was initiated.

PHASE 6: FOLLOW THROUGH
The Key Individual and the Team Sustaining,
the Province and the Order Doing

The team goes into the sustaining stage when the process regarding the terminal point of change is defined. The key team defines the end, the phases, time deadlines, who will do what by when, and how the change can be sustained. Then it is freed as the momentum is under way and there's continuity in the entire organisation.

If the change process fits the change needs, then there is continuity as the process proceeds. If the change process is not sufficient to

meet the change needs, if there is a lack of satisfaction within the
order as to how the change is moving, or a lack of ownership of the
change process, then the question of whether or not second-order
change is required must be dealt with. It is not uncommon, at this
point, for any organisation facing second-order change to revert to
Phase 2 in which the key individual has to convince the team of the
necessity of second-order change and deal with its members' denial
and dodging in this regard.

PHASE 7: SUSTAINING
The Key Individual, Team, Province and Order Sustaining

When there is a new relationship between the order and those with
whom it ministers, when its stakeholders come to accept the

*In organisational change,
people change at different
paces.*

changed state and interact with it in
the new way, and when the structures and review processes are in
place, then sustaining has occurred.
In the initial stages of sustaining, a good deal of energy must be
devoted to ensuring that the change has worked, by monitoring
feedback, both from within and outside the order. Feedback is
available through attention to each of the four levels.

In summary, the seven phases of change provide a framework for
one clear fact of experience, that in organisational change people
change at different paces. This is partly as a result of access to information. The seven phases framework is built on the sequence that
when one party is aware of the need for change and begins initiating change, another party may be caught unawares and typically
responds by denying and dodging.

The case we are following in this chapter is interesting for two reasons. First, the denying, dodging and doing stages of change are
clearly evident over an extensive period. Each stage lasted several
years and required distinctively separate interventions. Second, the
three successive provincials effectively worked from an organisational levels framework, without being aware of such a framework
– beginning with a Level IV strategy intervention, and when that
ran into difficulty turning to intervene on Level I, which naturally
flowed into Level II training and later led to a Level III policy formation process and a Level IV strategic plan. Over the eighteen years,

while many first-order changes took place, the deeper second-order, cultural change evolved through the planned change process.

CONCLUSIONS

Change involves a letting go of familiar and accepted ways of seeing and doing things. It can take a lot for us to acknowledge that change is needed – up to that we deny the need for change. Then we dodge it and leave it to others. When that position cannot be sustained, we begin to see what is required, what needs changing, how, when, at what cost, etc. As the relevant changes are made, they need to be sustained so that the change survives. This framework adds necessary detail to the unfreezing-changing-refreezing change model, by specifying the initial reactions to change, by showing how members of an order can be at different stages of the change process, and how in an order change moves through the key individual, teams and communities and the province towards the entire order.

An organisation development consultant can facilitate the individual provincial, the team and the province attend to the processes within the change effort and identify and work through the stages and phases of the change. Such an approach allows the members of the province to understand what is going on and develop the key diagnostic and problem-solving skills to manage change themselves. The consultant collaborates with the members of the province in designing the particular activities that help deal with the issues of each stage and move the individual, the team and the province through the change phases.

CHAPTER 7

Groups in the Renewal Process

As we have seen in a chapter 4, membership of a group is a particular element in the process of change and re-education. There are two approaches to using groups as mechanisms for helping advance a renewal process. One approach is to renew existing groups, particularly teams and communities. The other approach is to set up task forces or committees to work on particular aspects of the change. In this chapter team building will be examined and then the use of task forces as mechanisms for change discussed.

TEAM-BUILDING IN COUNCILS

Teams perform four functions (Figure 7-1). They set goals and priorities. They analyse and allocate work according to roles and responsibilities of the team members. They manage their team process, that is how the team works. They build and maintain the working relationships among the members. When a team takes time to reflect on itself, these four purposes are present. Team-building has as its purpose the strengthening of these functions.

It is important in team-building activities to use these four purposes in the order in which they are presented. Interpersonal problems can be a consequence of unclear goals, procedures, responsibilities or roles. Procedural problems can grow from a vagueness about responsibilities, roles and goals. There can be problems about roles and responsibilities because of a lack of clarity about team goals and priorities.

There are different perspectives on each of these purposes. The team leader typically is most concerned about getting the work done effectively, while members may be more concerned about their position, expectations and their contribution to the overall venture. The outcome is that these are in harmony to the extent that the work is done effectively. A consultant or facilitator working

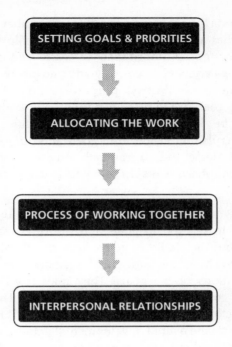

Figure 7-1
Function of teams

with the team is generally working on clarity of communication, areas of agreement or unclarity, problem-solving and decision-making and other areas of effective group process.

Setting Goals and Priorities

While in most cases councils work democratically and are sensitive to areas of consensus or disagreement, that should not be taken for granted. Therefore, it is useful to articulate some basic issues about goals and priorities in teams. First, the goals of the team must be clear and have an adequate measure of agreement among the team members. Time spent by a team articulating goals and building consensus around priorities is time well spent. If there is no clarity or agreement, then the team is likely to experience fundamental difficulties. A second issue relates to the role of leadership in setting priorities. Does the leader set the goals and priorities or does the team decide? How much freedom do the members have in formulating the agenda? What is expected of team members? Generally, it is accepted that a leader can facilitate ownership by acting in a democratic manner. Authoritarian or *laissez-faire* behaviours are found to be less effective in creating an atmosphere in which team members come to own the basic purposes and direction of the team endeavour. If goals are to provide a useful aid to motivation, then they need to be democratically conceived. A third issue revolves around distinguishing vision from goals and differentiating types of goals – strategic and operational, long-term and short-term. Goal-setting emphasises results to be achieved, rather than things to be done.

Consultants working with a council typically attend to many of the above issues in relation to goals and priorities. They may raise questions about the clarity of goals, agreement and ownership of priorities, and how the individual members understand each other's definitions of the goals. They may question the team's awareness of consequences of decisions, and challenge their commitment to action. They may reflect to the council how particular decisions fit into the overall developmental pattern, i.e. are congruent with vision and charism, respond to the demands of the environment, and are realistic in terms of resources.

A key issue for provincials and general councils frequently centres around the tension between allocating time for working on development and ongoing administrative demands. Council meetings tend to be dominated by the exigencies of current issues, particularly problems, and can become the focus of a council's energy. At the same time, the broader developmental issues of where the province is going in terms of its charism, the demands of the external environment, and the limitations of present and future resources, require attention. A tension can arise in the council from the pressure of the multiplicity of problems to be solved and the nagging feeling that the group should not be so caught up in such issues and should be engaging in developmental planning. In one case, a consultant sensed this tension from how the council was selecting its agenda for the meeting, raised the question and facilitated the council to look at its priorities as a council. The outcome was a restructuring of the regular council meetings in a manner that allowed for time to be spent on a cycle of systematic review of the major policy issues facing the congregation, and at the same time allocate an appropriate amount of time on concrete operational issues.

Analysing and Allocating the Work – Roles and Responsibilities

The effective team works from goals to methods of achieving them. Goals need to be broken down into tasks, with responsibilities and roles defined. The leader assigns and allocates work to the team and to individual members. Who is to do what? When? Where? How? The work steps not only must be understood, but their relation to the goals be perceived. In the team overall, one might expect to find an equal distribution of work, with the best use of talent and an effective union of individual effort to achieve unified team effort. In some councils work is allocated on a portfolio basis, that is, council members undertake responsibilities in terms of apostolic areas, i.e. primary education, secondary education, formation. Some general councils, which have a wide international responsibility, use geographical areas as the basis. On these issues of analysing and allocating work to be done, the consultant may attend to how to look at the relevant issues and provide frameworks for handling particular ones.

> *Effectiveness involves having processes which help the team achieve its goals and which do not block collective action.*

A team found itself overburdened by the need to discuss many issues, in that an endless spiral of meetings developed that sapped energy and created stress. A consultant introduced the notion of responsibility charting – a technique by which different roles and responsibilities are mapped out in relation to specific tasks – so that the members could clarify what needed to be done by whom on key issues and what roles other members wanted or needed to play on those issues.

Process – How the Team Works

Process refers to *how* things are done. Effectiveness involves having processes that help the team achieve its goals and that are not dysfunctional or blocking collective action. Process in a team typically points to areas such as: communication among members, role functions, leadership style, problem-solving and decision-making procedures, cultural assumptions, norms, how conflict is managed, ways of dealing with change, relations with other teams, and how the team develops. Teams have a developmental, collective personality. There are mature teams and immature teams. A sign of a mature team is that it can detect and learn from its mistakes. This requires an ability and skill in reviewing its own process in a way that does not resort to patterns of inference, attribution and the placing of blame. A further process issue is an effective use of time spent in meetings.

For consultants, the critical issue is how the process enables the team to achieve its task. It is relatively simple to intervene on process issues in their own terms, but to do so misses the point. What is of use to the team is what guides consultants. It may not be necessary for a particular team to maintain an equality of participation in every discussion, or that a discernment process be used. Consultants have to judge what interventions are relevant to the tasks at hand, and so may have to lay aside their own particular preferences of what an 'effective' group is, so as not to sidetrack the team into process issues that are consultant-centred rather than team-centred.

A consultant facilitated a decision-making process in which the central issue was less about the decision itself and more about the anxiety and fear of the decision in the group. The group spent some time focusing on the key forces driving and restraining the change; they prayed about the decision, shared the fruits of their prayer and made the decision with peace and relief. When it came to discussing implementation, the anxieties and fears surfaced. The group was enabled to face these anxieties and resolve the emotional effect the decision was having on one of its members. What was critical for the group was that the emotional agenda was handled gently, while at the same time not allowed to paralyse the group or renege on the decision.

Interpersonal Relationships

Teams are basically about people working together to achieve common goals. This is a complex process because the human person is complex, and there are multiple layers of complexities when individuals attempt to co-operate in a common endeavour. Individuals have their personal goals in being a team member, and these have to be harmonised with the team goals. The overall team goals must be inclusive of individual personal goals, so that participation in the team provides some occasion of personal development for individuals. A further complexity is found in the differences in people's approaches to working together. These approaches have been conceptualised in many ways. The Myers-Briggs Type Indicator is an example of how personality descriptions have been applied to interpersonal working relations.

Acceptance and trust are core elements in effective interpersonal working relationships. Acceptance requires a recognition of difference and an effort to understand the role of difference in a collective endeavour through active listening. Team members need to learn to trust each other to the degree that promotes the team activity. Openness of communication, a willingness to confront interpersonal problems, an ability in the team to listen to feelings and to accept each others' experience, are essential for effective team development. An added dimension for religious teams is the ability to form a community of faith, so that the individual's faith experience can be brought to the team's collective problem-solving and decision-making efforts. On these issues the consultant frequently attempts to, a) model some behaviours that are central to the team – active listening, nonjudgemental feedback, confrontation, process awareness, b) provide a safe environment in which difficult interpersonal issues can be dealt with.

As part of a three-day annual team planning and review meeting, an evening session was spent on the Myers-Briggs Type Indicator. The consultant led the group through the Indicator, and with the group's permission charted the group's perceived types. He then interviewed the team leader in front of the group on his own perceived strengths and weaknesses in terms of his type. For instance, his preference for extroverted intuition was explored in terms of his habit of talking out the possibilities that were passing through his head, so that the team learned to ask him if he were issuing instructions or simply thinking aloud. In this way, certain tensions were aired and the psychological contract between them clarified.

TASK FORCES AND COMMISSIONS

The ongoing renewal of contemporary church and religious life typically involves utilisation of groups to create or implement policy.

Provincials may have several permanent commissions or groups which monitor, administer or advise on policy on particular areas of ministry, such as education, health-care, continuing formation or the development of ministry. On occasions, temporary task forces or committees may be set up to investigate and advise on some particular aspect of ministry or living and submit a report to a provincial. Such a use of groups, whether through permanent or temporary groups, is a key mechanism for (a) the development of policy and (b) the generation of commitment to change by participation in the process of policy formulation. The contribution to the development of policy comes through the involvement of a variety of selected individuals who are invited to be members of these groups and who contribute from their experience and expertise. The groups help form commitment by the range of participation and through the consultation the groups may hold with the wider membership of the order or province.

As we have seen, all working groups have to deal with two areas – task and relational, that is, issues around the work to be done and the working relationships of the members. These two areas each comprise issues of content and process. In the task area, *content* refers to what is to be done and *process* how it is to be done. In the relational area, *content* refers to the group members' work with one another and *process* how the group works.

The Task Area

For commissions, task forces and committees, the task content is the work to be done, whether it be policy formulation or advice to a superior and whether it be in a specialised area of ministry or an overview of ministries. The starting point for any working group is the clarity of the task – what it is that the group is being asked to do, what the limits of the task are, what the time scale is, etc. The group will have to work at ensuring that it understands its task and clarifying members' assumptions and interpretations of what it means.

Task process refers to how the group goes about its task. In my experience, a most valuable way of approaching the sort of task that groups like commissions, task forces or committees are assigned is to begin by conceiving what the members of the group would like to see achieved by the end of its term or the completion of the task.

For example, a consultant may put an exercise to the group such as, 'Picture yourselves handing over to the next commission in three years' time; what state do you want the ministry to be in at that time? What are the core issues you will have to address and would like to have resolved or moved on a bit in your term of office?' Some personal reflection and prayer time for each individual member would be assigned, after which the group would meet to hear the individual visions and begin to build consensus. An exercise such as this enables the group to look at the big picture at the outset and not get sucked into detail too soon. It facilitates the group taking hold of its task and setting the direction of the work. An approach which begins at the desired future and then looks at the present to see what it is that needs to be done in order to reach that desired future ensures a sense of purpose and helps keep any task group focused.

The Relational Area

For the advisory group, commission or task force, there are three key systemic relationships – relations within the group itself, relations with the provincial, and relations with the other members of the province.

Relations within the group require an ability to work together in such a way that the work gets done and that the individual members contribute actively to the task and to the group. Group members have different areas of expertise and competence. They have had different life experiences in ministry. There is typically a range of different personality types in any group. Understanding individual differences and how they contribute to the life and task of the group is the core of the relational content within the group.

Relations with the provincial require an initial dialogue on the nature and meaning of the task. The group needs to understand what provincials' desired future is and, if they don't have one, then to help them develop one! If a group develops policy away from what the provincial is comfortable with, then the result of the group's work may well be ignored or not followed through. Therefore, the relational content of the relationship between the group and the provincial – the agreed meaning of the assigned task and its progress – needs to be continuously articulated and communicated so that there are no surprises. Provincials know what the

group is doing and the groups knows what the provincial is thinking and doing.

Relations with the province is perhaps the most neglected relational
area. How often do we see the work of commissions and task forces
perceived as irrelevant and ignored unless the provincial personally
reinforces it? When formal consultation with the wider system is
part of the group's task, how often is it such a painful experience
that it creates a resolve never to serve on a commission again! The
relational content of the relationship between the group and the
membership of the province is essential if the group's work is to act
as a mechanism for the renewal of the whole system.

The processes of managing each of these three key relationships are
critical for the work of any task force or commission, whether permanent or temporary. The group must consciously take account of
the existence of these relationships and monitor how they are at the
different stages of the group's work. Because these relationships are
systemic, they have a relationship with each other; that is, the relationship with the provincial affects the relations within the group
and the relationship with the province and so on. Neglect of one set
of relationships will have a negative affect on the other sets.

The focus has been on content and process issues of task forces and
commissions, under the headings of task and relational, with a
view to directing attention on how the work of commissions can be
improved. Any change on the lines suggested above, however, are
improvements within an existing frame of reference, that is, an
adjustment of a present way of approaching the work of task forces
and commissions. What is required is a transformation of those
very frames of reference whereby a different concept of task forces
and commissions is formulated with different values articulated
and consequent implications for the behaviour and process of these
commissions. Such a transformation comes about through conceiving them as learning groups – both within themselves and as a
learning mechanism for the rest of the system.

BEING A LEARNING GROUP

A learning group is one which consciously attends to the dynamics
of its own learning. Accordingly, attention is given not only to the
group dynamics – such as process issues regarding communication,

decision-making, forms of meetings, etc., – but also to articulating what the group is learning about its task and about how to go about its task. The key elements of being a learning group in a religious context is the deliberate focus on and attention to the spiritual dynamics of the group.

There is a continuing development of awareness and skills in integrating the dynamics of working groups with the dynamics of shared spirituality, 'the contemplative life in prayer and the contemplative life in the group meeting'. Such an integration involves building on the faith experience of the individual members and then helping form the commission into a community of faith. This may be done by some faith-sharing activities in the initial meeting so as to set an atmosphere, norms and psychological contract between the members so that the work of the commission is such that the Word of God is allowed influence and direct it. That faith-sharing then becomes an integral part of how the group works.

As the group goes about its work – identifying issues, selecting options, reaching consensus on proposals, goals or action – it must build into its process activities of problem-analysis and problem-solving, alternative solution generation, reflection on the experience of those activities, taking that reflection to prayer, studying what is emerging in the group, questioning assumptions and taking it back to prayer. The quality of process and relationships must be such that the Holy Spirit can work in the group. Reflection on the process involves attending to when the group is in desolation or consolation and noting the movements of the Good or Bad Spirit.

> *Reflection on the process involves attending to when the group is in desolation or consolation and noting the movements of the good or bad spirit.*

Developing a quality of group life in a commission where the cognitive and analytical work of the group is harmonised with a shared faith which attends to the movements of the Spirit in the group requires that each member attend to the movements in his or her own heart and mind. It involves listening to oneself, noting one's own reactions to what is said by other members, questioning one's own assumptions in the light of that reaction and in the light of others' views. It involves questioning others' assumptions to hear and

understand what lies behind what they are saying. This is particularly important when words like 'community', 'togetherness' 'mission' are used – words that we frequently and mistakenly assume to
have the same meanings for everyone! Questioning and helping
articulate assumptions is not unlike the sort of testing understanding activity which a therapist, spiritual director or fellow community
member does in the process of a therapy or spiritual direction session or community sharing. At the same time it has a different focus
and aim, which is not to clarify feelings but to build mutual understanding and new shared assumptions in order to advance the task.
It is a form of task-focused dialogue.

In one consultation to a commission, a consultant gave a group the
task of articulating how it was going to work and of formulating a
sort of charter for itself. When the group returned, one member
reported that the group had not really got into the task, had chatted
a good deal and done some other more immediate business, such as
electing a chairperson and secretary. She then said that it was probably the post-lunch-early afternoon blues that had created this situation. This was an example of not questioning assumptions about
what was happening in the group. Raising the question of what
was happening that the group was not working on its task could
well have brought out that the task was unclear, that it was threatening or that the other members did not know how to go about it.
Consequently, that particular commission was not able to engage in
a learning process in that situation.

Being a learning group involves pausing to see where convergences
and divergences are and what they mean, and facing ambiguities,
anxieties, differences, feelings of alienation or boredom because
these are what can thwart a group's work. If the group can learn to
bring these into the open and deal with them, then it is learning a
more effective way of achieving its task than if these continue to
have an unacknowledged negative effect on the group. In the same
vein, noting the movements of consolation and desolation, the
temptations to fold under pressure and follow the Bad Spirit, are
critical if the group is be effective in doing its work. In addition,
these typically all exist in the wider system and are part of why
change is so difficult, so if the commission can learn about bringing
them into the open in a safe environment and dealing with them,

then it can be a significant mechanism for facilitating change in the wider system.

One practical way a commission can control the quality of its process to facilitate being a learning group is by distinguishing different types of meetings and process. There may be times when the group meets for two hours and receives reports, looks at data and plans a next step. There may be other meetings which take up a half day, a whole day or a weekend, where there is time and space to study the material in more depth, take time for prayer, reflection and review and allow the Spirit to inform the group. Another concrete tool is to appoint a group member to take responsibility for the group's learning process. Just as the group may appoint a chairperson and secretary, it may also designate a member to ensure reflection time is not whittled away and that the group regularly takes time to review its process and learning. Such roles may rotate. Occasionally it may be useful, particularly for the longer meetings, to have a facilitator, who may act in a consultant-facilitator-group spiritual director role.

Attention to what the group is learning can be structured around some central questions. One such model would be the following sequences of questions and their accompanying answers: 'I have thought about ... and I think that ... I have prayed about ... and sense that ... I have listened to others and now think that ... I am aware in myself that ... What I think we are being called to is...' These sorts of questions can help a group do its analytical work and note what is being thought. It can help the group change levels and, having done its analytical work, go deeper into the world of the Spirit, and sense what is emerging from prayer. Having sensed what is happening in individuals and the group, the group may hear the call to a particular action, which then must be prayed about and confirmation sought. Clearly, this is not a logical or linear sequence and not to be oversimplified.

HELPING THE PROVINCE LEARN

One of the reasons why a process, such as creating a learning group, is important is that it can act as a model for the rest of the system. If commissions meet, draw up recommendations and pass them on to a provincial for approval and implementation which doesn't happen, it may well be partly due to how the group has worked, how the group relates to the provincial and how it relates to the province. In

The task of a commission is not only to produce policy but also to enable the rest of the system to change and learn.

the context of the change required in the church, whether in general or in specific ministries, there are major issues at stake for religious orders. No longer can change be an option. Accordingly, there are enormous responsibilities on those commissions and task forces which are established to help move change forward. It isn't acceptable now, after so many years of using groups and attempting to manage change, to set up commissions and have them do work which is then ignored or is not effective.

In the system, change is typically marked by no small amount of fear and anxiety, insecurity about the future, ambivalence, conflict about whether change is wanted or not and conflict about what should change, to name a few of the common issues. Individuals and other human systems require the presence of a sense of psychological safety in order to move from the security of the present to a changed state. Accordingly, the management of change requires that such a sense of psychological safety be created to help individuals and groups face and deal with the anxieties which accompany change. Individuals or groups can hold a community or province to ransom and block any substantive change or discussion about change. Provincials and their councils spend lots of time discussing how individuals and communities are blocked and how they might help change move forward. The change process typically fails to engage the actual integration of prayer and action in dealing with the struggles which accompany change. If prayer was directed towards the hurts which exist in the system, and if a group or community could prayerfully face the real issues which are actual forces in a situation, then change could genuinely be led by the Spirit.

Therefore, modelling is one significant way in which the work of commissions and task forces can contribute to large system change. If the members of a commission work in such a way so as to deal productively with the fears, anxieties, tensions, trepidations, uncertainties, conflicts, the enormity of the task and the complexity of the issues, the insecurity of the future, and live through the transition period, and if they can do that through their shared faith and the spirituality of the system, then the commission can act as a learning model for the whole system. Therefore, the task of a commission is, not only to produce policy, but also to enable the rest of the system change and learn. In organisation development, this process is referred to as a 'parallel learning structure', that is, a structure whereby a commission consciously works in a way which is different from what typically happens in the system. In the normal working of teams, conflict is typically avoided and not taken seriously to prayer, then a commission which works in an atypical manner can bring what it has learned from the experience to the rest of the system, particularly since this atypical behaviour stems from core religious values and attention to the process of the group's spiritual experience.

The question behind the above proposals is how does a large complex system such as a religious order learn? Such a question encourages reflection on operative theories of learning. One dominant learning model is the rational-empirical model in which documents articulating policy are presented for all to assent to and follow, much in the way teachers present material in class for students to accept. Yet from our experience, we see the flaws in such an approach. It doesn't help people deal with the fears which might accompany a proposal for change. It doesn't take account of how individuals identify with groups and are socialised into the culture of those groups, and that changing culture requires more than an edict to change collective assumptions and habits. We have internalised newer learning models from our experiences in spiritual direction and therapy and haven't yet developed their potential in applying them to the management of change.

The core of an effective approach to learning and change is one which helps deal with anxiety and fear of change. If the commissions and task forces work as parallel learning structures in such a way that encourages learning about fear and anxiety, then provinces have a mechanism for helping that learning be actively available.

> *An effective approach to learning and change helps deal with anxiety and fear of change.*

Edgar Schein articulates four assumptions in this regard:

(1) 'One cannot ask others to learn something new if one has not learned something new oneself.' Therefore, from this assumption it can be seen that if a commission has learned about how to understand and manage the conflicts and anxieties in change, it can help the rest of the system do so.

(2) 'Learning in this complex area involves stepping outside one's own culture before one can discover the limitations of one's present culture and possibilities inherent in other cultures.' This assumption focuses on how working in a manner which builds on shared spiritual experience and attends to process in a way which the rest of the system rarely does, opens up ways of working with the rest of the system.

(3) 'Anxieties inherent in this new learning situation are only manageable if they are shared and managed jointly in a group which is accountable for the ultimate welfare of the organisation.' In this assumption is the argument that when groups are commissioned with the task of developing a particular aspect of policy, they be accountable for how the change process works.

(4) 'Learning will not be spread across the entire organisation unless a change/transition management group is created which will be accountable for organisational learning.' What this assumption is focusing on is that commissions and task forces be given the task of consciously helping develop learning in the rest of the system. This can only happen if the commission itself goes through a learning process by working in a way which deals with the difficult issues in a manner congruent with the spiritual and psychological dynamics of the group.

CONCLUSIONS

This chapter has focused on the process of using groups in renewal. A team- building model which structures the issues teams have to deal with, in an order that works from goals through work allocation, through process, to relationships, was presented. A case for the transformation of the role of task forces and commissions in the work of policy formulation and renewal by turning them into learning groups was made. Learning groups are those which attend to their own learning and then act as vehicles for the organisation's learning. Such a transformation is integrally linked to attention to

the spiritual dynamics of a group and by modelling a way of working which consciously deals with questioning assumptions, facing
fears in the context of a shared faith perspective, and taking its
experiences to prayer.

CHAPTER 8

Provincial Assemblies

Many religious orders have used and are using assemblies as a means of helping the development of the renewal process. Assemblies are large meetings, where most members of a province come together for several days to discuss policy issues and set some form of strategic direction for the future. They can last anything from one day to two weeks, though they typically tend to be two or three days in duration.

What an assembly is essentially about is that, by bringing the whole system into a room, a large system attempts to create a shared sense of direction and a commitment to that direction. In an assembly the whole system is put on view – its past (where it has come from, its history, traditions, successes and failures ...), its present (what is happening now, how the past, present and future are perceived, its members' experiences, feelings ...) and its future (where it wants to go, where it can go ...). The past, present and future are represented by having most of the members of the province present and by the ages of those members. The traditional ministries of the province are present through the members who have worked in them and built them up over many years. The future of the province is represented by the younger members. The present is represented by the age diversity, the present concerns and the desires for the future. In many assemblies the province's lay colleagues are present and represent the growing partnership between religious and laity. Through the work of the assembly, the members then can view the total picture and respond to it (Figure 8-1).

The generic purposes of an assembly are to enable those who have a stake in the province and its ministries to discuss shared desires and intentions, take responsibility for their own plans, and implement a shared vision. There are five simple tasks which underlie the

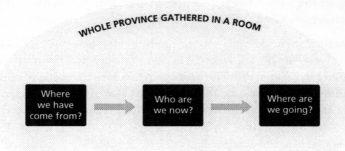

Figure 8-1
The Provincial Assembly

work of an assembly – review the past, explore the present, create an ideal future scenario, identify common ground and make action plans.

One technique used to elicit a shared perspective on the past is through the communal drawing of a history line whereby events which are judged to be significant by the members present are, first named, and secondly, their significance articulated. A community of meaning is enforced by a public statement of the significance of the stories which have helped form the province. A central element of this community of meaning is the acknowledgement of events which created hurt and division. It may be important for the group to enact a liturgy of reconciliation and healing in which the hurts of the past are acknowledged and forgiveness sought and given.

In the focus on the present, the external and internal trends which are shaping the present reality are identified. In the contemporary world there are many external forces which are creating change, whether religious like it or not. There are also internal forces which can be characterised by the age structure of the province and the changing nature of ministry. The assembly must immerse itself in the present reality in order to own the necessity and inevitability of change. This activity may create considerable anxiety and fear in members of the assembly. A significant aspect of the process of naming the present reality is the prayer and prayerful reflection which seeks to find God in the present reality.

In creating an ideal future scenario, the province is putting itself ten to twelve years hence, where it is asking itself what it would like to be doing in that period. The process in this activity is one of creating common themes for a shared movement into the future. It is identifying potential projects which the province can undertake which will mark the province's efforts to shape the future it wants. In this respect, the process is understood in terms of the spirituality of desiring, and of owning common desires.

An assembly is a complex interplay between the four organisational levels, as individuals take stock of their relationship to the order (Level I), work in small groups to create a shared vision of the future (Level II), and the many different groups, teams, communities, backgrounds are co-ordinated to form a unified whole which must be capable of creating common ground to move to the future (Level III), so that the order may better exercise ministry according to its charism (Level IV). Through the process of an assembly, individuals unfreeze and change, groups may unfreeze and change, as a prelude to the whole system unfreezing and changing.

The core process of an assembly involves inter-level dynamics (Figure 8-2). Each individual participant is invited to reflect on particular issues and themes, share the fruit of this in a small group

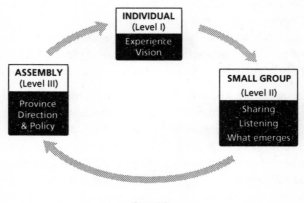

Figure 8-2
Process of an Assembly

and then bring those two experiences to the assembly gathered in plenary. What happens in the plenary may then be brought back to the small groups for further consideration and for individual reflection. These processes continually involve crossing boundaries from individual to small group to large group.

In an assembly individuals spend time getting in touch with their own vision and desires for the future. Individuals bring their vision and desires to the small groups, share, listen and hear the desires and visions of others and then join the plenary where a province-wide perspective is viewed, perhaps through posters, collages, etc. At each step something new is created. The outcome is not the sum of every individual contribution. Each individual reflection and sharing has helped form what emerges. If individuals or groups begin to complain that their view is not represented and get aggravated, it may be a sign that the participants do not feel psychologically safe. Then there may be a need to retrace some steps to address the desolation and build sufficient psychological safety for the members to form a community which can build common ground in consolation.

> *The process of developing common ground is messy.*

The process of developing common ground is messy. It involves creating a space to develop inner freedom, listening to others and then creating out of what is heard. It may be that the assembly goes through phases of development. Because the assembly is not a regular event, the large group has to *form* itself, build trust and a way of being together in loving, co-operative, prayerful relationships to engage in the task at hand. It may go through a *storming* stage where the harshness of reality – the need for change, substantive disagreements among members, fear, real pain and hurt – is faced. If it is faced honestly and in faith and love, then the assembly can create *norms* of being able to be together in a prayerful discerning mode and *perform* its task. Then there is *termination* as the assembly ends and the participants prepare to return to their apostolates and communities.

The following case presents an outline of an assembly of a province of a congregation of sisters which aimed at developing ownership of its general chapter's mandates.

CASE

The Assembly opened in the evening with the provincial's address, in which she outlined the shifts which had taken place in the province in recent years, highlighting, for example, the movement from large communities to small, from working for people to working with people and a focus on developing leaders. She presented the directions from the general chapter and said that she was formally asking for a mandate to implement a movement towards greater solidarity with marginalised people and the development of a spirituality of action-reflection. She emphasised that while everyone was being called to these directions, not everyone was called in the same way. After the provincial's address, the facilitator invited the assembly participants to take a few minutes in silence to reflect on 'What is present for me?' and then individuals shared responses.

The following morning, the facilitator directed the participants to enter into a concrete experience of being with marginalised people. They took personal time to do that and then spent some time in small groups sharing and listening. They were instructed to give time to reflecting and commenting on the small group process so as to help develop as sense of process. From the personal reflection and group sharing on experience with marginalised people, each group developed an image which was expressed on paper and posted on the wall of the assembly hall. The posted images were the focus of the Liturgy of the Word at the Eucharist as the participants took time to read the posters, ask questions of the groups which had written them and share their responses. The posted images expressed the voice of the province. Finally, that evening the participants met in their small groups to explore what action they might take in response to the call for greater solidarity with marginalised people. The following morning some of these proposed actions were shared in the plenary session.

In mid-morning on the second day, the assembly was asked to spend time identifying the shifts which had taken place in the province's ministry over the past ten years, with regard to the *what* of ministry, the *how* of ministry, the *way of life* which surrounds ministry and the *consciousness* or patterns of thinking about ministry. Each group was limited to identifying three such shifts. The small groups did the work and presented their findings and posted them on the wall of the assembly hall. As had been done previously, the participants spent time studying the reported shifts and then attempting to get an overall sense of the province as it was being expressed.

The consultant took some time to map the flow of the assembly's process so far, focusing on (a) beginning with the experience of marginalised people, taking those experiences to prayer and to fellow sisters and listening to them, (b) how from that some shape was put on those experiences through the images, and then (c) time was spent trying to identify patterns and shifts in the province's experience of ministry over the past ten years. In the consultant's view, these three processes provided an articulation of the province's path and a sense of the progress of the journey and the key themes of that journey. Now there would be a shift to moving towards looking to the future, to a new century. If things continued the way they were going, without any significant intervention, the inevitable or projected future scenario could be painted. If an alternative scenario were to be painted, one expressed in terms of charism, the thrust of the congregation and the changing society, a desired future could be articulated which would be the focus of meaningful direction and leadership. The consultant concluded, 'If you don't know where you are going, it doesn't matter where you end up. If you don't work at where you're going, you may end up somewhere else, and if you don't have a future you want, you'll end up in someone else's desired future.'

The assembly was commissioned then to work on an expression of its desired future, the images of that future and what it is in the present which needs to change in order to get to that future. Following the now established process, individuals took time for personal prayer and reflection; the small groups then worked from the individuals' work and then posted the fruit of their work on the walls of the assembly hall. The assembly in plenary studied what was posted and attempted to get a sense of the province, and responded to what was posted.

The plenary meeting on the morning of the third day was the turning point of the assembly. For over an hour, individuals responded and reacted to the material on the walls – sharing feelings of anxiety, depression, apprehension and hope. Clarification of core constructs like the relationship between unity and diversity, accountability, the ramifications of the choices for community living and the kinds of ministry were made. The assembly formally endorsed the provincial's mandates, and in the words of a scripture text, which became a theme, the province 'set its face towards Jerusalem'.

The following day, the fourth and final day of the assembly, was devoted to taking the three core themes of the assembly and identifying what steps could be taken at community and provincial level to sustain a personal and corporate thrust towards these objectives. The small groups selected particular themes, worked on them, formed cluster groups with other groups, and presented the fruit of their work to the assembly. Time was given to the small groups to terminate, and some time was devoted to community groups to meet and make some preliminary plans for following up the work of the assembly.

At one point there was inter-group interaction. Such boundary crossing is significant in enabling individuals to strengthen their ego-function by developing responsibility for the roles they have to take in different settings and in taking personal authority in exercising those roles. Individuals were challenged by the structure of the assembly to examine their perspectives on the general chapter's mandates in the light of their identity as sisters and so take responsibility for their responses to those mandates as the expression of their bonding to the congregation. They also learned something of how to think in terms of province. When the small groups brought their work to the assembly hall and posted it on the wall, and the participants spent time wandering around studying each poster, they were then asked to sit and become aware of what was striking them overall. Consistently through the assembly, individuals reported that the statement by the facilitation team, 'This is the province' was very powerful.

The small groups functioned as temporary systems to bridge the psychological gap between the individual and the assembly in plenary. These small groups operated as 'parallel learning structures' in that (a) the process as designed focused on the spirituality of 'action-reflection', itself one of the core elements of the general chapter and the agenda of the assembly, and (b) the members of the assembly not only had very positive experiences of the process of sharing and working, but more significantly saw them as models of how local communities might function.

Articulating a desired future is the prerequisite for managing planned change as it is in the light of a desired future that the present reality can be viewed and assessments of what kinds of changes, and in what parts of the system, can be made. Accordingly, the focus in the assembly of articulating a desired future, out of which the movement for change in the present would be grounded, was essential.

The challenge in any change process is that in creating disconfirmation and anxiety, the change agents must provide sufficient psychological safety so that those required to change are not paralysed by the disconfirmation and anxiety. What is necessary for movement to occur is that the disconfirmation and anxiety be experienced and viewed in a manner which shows that change is possible, desirable and manageable. The early stages of the assembly's process were designed to create a sufficient degree of psychological safety to balance any negative effects of disconfirmation. The process began with a focus on experience and sharing in the small groups, which participants reported as being 'gentle' and 'non-threatening'. The participants themselves expressed surprise at the level of trust and intimacy which developed in the small groups in a short space of time. At the same, the content of the work was challenging and the crossing of boundaries into the assembly in plenary kept a sharpness to the proceedings.

The disconfirming information was evidenced in (a) the changing nature of the society in which the sisters minister, (b) the demands of the general chapter, and (c) the age structure of the province with its consequent anxiety about the future of the congregation and its ministries. When the assembly's agenda moved to the topic of the province's desired future, and the challenge of change became more focused, the sense of psychological safety created in the small groups enabled individuals to face the question of what changes in the present would be required to move towards the desired future. The assembly appears to have been successful in unfreezing the province. It did this by focusing on disconfirming information, maintaining a sense of anxiety, while at the same time, creating an atmosphere of psychological safety in which the participants could look at difficult questions, map out general directions in which the province would go, and create a supportive climate in which the ongoing work of change would continue after the assembly. The core elements of the creation of such sufficient psychological safety were: (a) starting in a non-threatening manner with individual reflection on experience and structuring that process with plenty of time for participants to settle into the process, (b) at the same time, having as the content of the reflection on experience a core agenda of the assembly and of the broader change at issue, (c) the work in small groups which actually created a sense of safety for individuals to share their reflections.

In terms of the broad agenda of the congregation's thrust from the general chapter, the assembly worked on the process of unfreezing. The work of changing is the agenda of the province's leadership over the remainder of its term of office. In terms of a more specific agenda around the work of the assembly itself, the members were unfrozen with regard to the mandates. They moved into the changing phase in imaging past patterns, the desired future and what needed changing in the present to get to that future, and then began to set agendas in community groups as to how to refreeze and sustain the work of assembly in the back-home situation.

The change thrust in the congregation was not directed simply at a set of administrative or structural alterations with a view to strengthening religious life and ministry. It was aiming at a change of paradigm of what it is to be a religious sister in that congregation. The assembly attempted to take account of the difference between values and basic assumptions. First, it did so by attending to experience and taking account of some individuals' actual apprehensions, fears and anxieties about change which could inhibit the ideas and drive of those who were already committed to radical change, and limit the progress of change in the province. Secondly, the interdependence and inter-relationship between the four organisational levels was structured into the assembly's process so that all issues were consistently exposed to the small groups and the assembly in plenary. Experiences, perceptions and ideas were constantly brought to a more public arena and tested. In that way, the province as a unit could begin to see what assumptions it needed to change, and begin to take steps to change them. The enemy of such change is when experiences and perceptions are privately held and not exposed to public testing.

The significant dimension at this assembly was the presence of the associates as stakeholders of the province's charism and mission. An assembly is a complex interplay between the four organisational levels as individuals take stock of their relationship to the organisation, work in small groups to create policy, and the many different groups, teams, backgrounds, sub-cultures are co-ordinated to form a unified whole which must be capable of adapting to the demands of the external environment. Through the process of an assembly, individuals unfreeze and change, groups may unfreeze and change, as a prelude to the whole system unfreezing and changing.

CONCLUSIONS

In this chapter a framework for understanding provincial assemblies was presented. An assembly is a situation in which a whole system is brought into a room to create a shared sense of direction and a commitment to that direction. In a provincial assembly the whole system is put on view – its past (where it has come from, its history, traditions, successes and failures …), its present (what is happening now, how the past, present and future are perceived, its members' experiences, feelings …) and its future (where it wants to go, where it can go …). Through the work of the assembly, the members of a province then can view the total picture and respond to it.

The provincial assembly described in this chapter was one moment in the ongoing life of that province and the congregation, a moment when some key change issues were advanced. In the view of the members of the province, and in particular the leadership, the assembly was a definite success, both in terms of advancing policy and developing ownership for change. In attempting to understand the experience of the assembly described in this chapter, the concept of the four organisational levels in which the bonding relationship between an individual and the congregation, the efforts to create working ministry teams and apostolic community, the efforts to co-ordinate multiple ministries in a province, and the adaptation of the congregation to the changing world in the light of its charism, are inter-linked is particularly useful. The assembly as a complex social system gathered in one room acted as a catalyst in integrating the four levels around the core issues of the congregation's general chapter and its movement into the future.

CHAPTER 9

Consultation and Facilitation

A significant element in the whole process of organisation development is the role and function of those who are professionals in helping organisations manage change, i.e. consultants. Using professional help is frequently a significant element of a change process.
Individuals might attend a therapist as part of attempting to make a
change in their lives. Individual religious utilise spiritual direction
as a way of gaining perspective on God in their life. Managers and
religious superiors may seek legal or financial expertise. In the
course of renewal most religious orders have at some time or other
used a consultant – usually someone from outside the order who is
perceived to have an expertise that the order requires. Areas of
expertise have included facilitation skills, communications, spirituality, planning, social analysis and canon law. The process of getting outside help for a problem can be formal or informal; it can
involve seeking expert advice or being helped to decide for oneself.
All these helping models apply to organisational change.

What are consultants? Consultants are generally defined as people
whose expertise have been contracted by a client. They may be
external or internal to the organisation. The 'client' is the organisation or person affected by the consultation project. The consultation
relationship is typically a voluntary one between a professional
helper and a help-needing client, in which the consultant is
attempting to help the client solve some problem. The relationship
is perceived to be temporary by both parties and the consultant is
an outsider to the client's power system. Consultants, i.e. those who
come into organisations in a helping role, can fulfil a wide range of
roles from technical expert to process facilitator. Effective helping
involves helping in such a way that problems are solved.

It is a comparatively recent development for religious orders to use consultants. Commercial enterprises have been using consultants for much longer. Religious orders have begun learning to use consultants primarily through using them as facilitators for chapters. Facilitation is not the same as consultancy, rather one dimension of it.

RELIGIOUS ORDERS AS CLIENTS

In any form of helping relationship, the better one is at being helped, the more effective the relationship. Being good at being helped can involve many factors. One key factor is knowing what one wants from the relationship. While there is a key element of growth in this process, i.e. what one thinks one wants can change through the process, having goals at the outset is paramount. Goals must be on two levels. Firstly, there are goals for the province or the particular ministry which are the intended results of the consultation process. These are typically in terms of the direction the province wants to go over the coming decade or the normative changes that need to be made. Secondly, there are goals specifically related to the role of the consultant. These goals typically give attention to the issues under discussion. Why have a consultant? What kind of consultant to do what? How do we choose? What sort of skills do we want in the consultant? A second factor in being good at being helped is, therefore, an ability to learn from and with the consultant.

Why use external consultants? When and for what should consultants be used? What consultants? Are there skills we should develop for ourselves within the order or province? It seems at present that most chapters and very many meetings use external consultants as facilitators. (Designing and facilitating a process is one form of intervention that a consultant can utilise.) Some consultants use a particular form of process that is associated with their work. An order, in its decision to use a consultant, may be focused primarily on the consultant – 'We'll ask X and whatever she does is okay because having X is the important thing.' It may be the reverse where the process is all important and the person is secondary. Both approaches have their advantages and pitfalls. Process A that consultant X uses may or may not be what is needed. Consultant X may or may not have the skills to work with the order in what it needs to do at the present time. A consultant may be very good at one process that is successful at a particular stage of community renewal but it may not be appropriate for an earlier or later stage or for ministry renewal. A facilitator may not be the answer to the problem. In general, a blank cheque invitation to a consultant 'to facilitate our chapter' does not do justice to either the consultant or the religious order. Clarity on what is needed is as essential as in a decision to tender a building contract or consult a medical specialist.

CHOOSING A CONSULTANT

The relationship between consultant and client is a reciprocal one. Provincials need to know if this person or team is able to provide what they want. Consultants decide whether this is a group with which they want to work. Spiritual direction relationships are tentative for the first few sessions till both parties agree to proceed. In commercial consultation, the initial meetings between consultant and client are to see whether or not they will work together. It is only after extensive discussions that a contract is agreed. Frequently either of the two parties will decline the contract. The common practice in religious orders is to phone consultant after consultant, probably from a list obtained from another order, till someone agrees. The contract is sealed in the first few minutes – 'Will you facilitate our chapter?' There tends to be little exploratory discussion prior to a decision. There is no comparison between what several consultants might be offering. There is no real choice if one accepts the first positive response. If a community is undertaking some building work, it will be careful about which builder it chooses and will shop around to ensure it gets what it wants at the right price. It can appear that religious orders can seem to move from consultant to consultant and from process to process – 'We had X for our chapter last time; now we're having Y!' What assumptions are operative in a situation like that might be hard to uncover. If an individual is seen to be changing spiritual director or counsellor at regular intervals, then serious questions can justifiably be asked. If an order is moving from process to process, from consultant to consultant, what does that mean? Is it that the previous consultant has judged that he or she is not the appropriate person to work with this order in its current state of development? Is it that the provincial has decided to drop that particular consultant? If it is the latter, is it for incompetence? How is the decision to invite a consultant made? Of course if the consultant was brought in to simply facilitate a series of meetings, then, changing to another facilitator may be an uncomplicated procedure. The question as to the effect of yet another new process on the members of the meeting, or the long-term development of the order, might be asked. As in the case of spiritual direction or counselling, questions about follow-through and consistency can be validly posed. What is at issue is not whether facilitators or processes change or not, but what the under-lying reasoning is and the effect of that reasoning, especially if it is unquestioned.

MODELS OF CONSULTATION

There are different models of consultancy. The most common ones are those which are based on the expertise of the consultant. Two forms of the expert model can be described. One is called the 'med-ical' or 'doctor-patient' model. In this model the client typically pre-sents the situation to the expert who performs a diagnosis and pre-scribes a remedy, which the client then implements. The second type of expert consultancy is called the 'purchase' model. In this model expertise is purchased. The expert comes in and frequently does the job in person. Examples of this approach is when we get in an accountant to audit the accounts or a canon lawyer to assist in the formulation of constitutions.

Both these models are grounded in the authoritative expertise of the consultant. The authority is based on the relationship between someone with expertise and someone who is ignorant. Power is based on expertise. Such a relationship has its appropriateness and its faults. Its strength lies in having the expertise in areas of content where there is clear ignorance and no desire to invest in having the necessary skills. So we buy in electronics skills when equipment breaks down. In the doctor-patient model we are expected to follow the prescription of the expert who understands our illness. It has inherent pitfalls in that we are relying on an external diagnosis which may or may not be accurate. We may find ourselves having to return to the 'doctor' when the next 'illness' surfaces. We may never learn the skills to solve our own problems.

PROCESS CONSULTATION

There is a third helping model, process consultation. Edgar Schein, the creator of process consultation, defines it as 'a set of activities on the part of the consultant which help the client perceive, under-

stand and act upon process events that occur in the client's environment in order to improve the situation as defined by the client'
(1988, page 11). Schein's underlying assumptions are that managers
often do not know what is wrong in
an organisation and need a special
kind of help to understand what
their problems actually are. They

> *The 'process consultation'*
> *model is different from*
> *'expert' models.*

often don't know what kinds of help consultants can give, and so
need help in knowing what kind of help to seek. They need help in
being able to identify what needs improving and what doesn't.
They may want to solve the problems themselves but they need
help in deciding what to do. In process consultation, consultants
work jointly with managers so that the managers can learn to see
the problems for themselves, share in the understanding and be
actively involved in creating their own solutions.

On the basis of such assumptions, it can be seen that the process
consultation model is in direct contrast with traditional consultation models. These models are based on particular areas of consultant expertise which the client consults for advice and/or expert
problem-solving. Schein makes this comparison as he places the
process consultation approach in juxtaposition with the doctor-
patient model and the purchase model. Process consultants, in contrast, are experts in building effective helping relationships which
are contingent on working jointly with clients so that the clients can
solve their own organisational problems. Finally, process consultants pass on their skills to their clients so that, in essence, managers
become process consultants in their own organisations. Schein
argues that the process consultation approach to helping constitutes authentic organisation development because it is genuinely
client-centred and follows the client's needs through the consultation process. This is contrasted with other helping models in which
the consultant predesigns a set of interventions and the client follows the consultant's interventions.

For process consultants to work with religious orders, they must be
able to work with the kind of organisation a religious order is. This
involves, at minimum, a knowledge of the values and culture. For
example, decisions may be made which, while they might not make
sense when viewed in financial terms, may be the perceived calling

of the order to radical ministry in keeping with its vocation in the church. External consultants to religious clients require a sensitivity to that aspect of the culture and an awareness of the role of prayer in decision-making. For process consultants to be maximally involved, they need to be skilled in facilitating prayerful decision-making. Frequently, lay external consultants work closely with an internal committee so as to enhance sensitivity and compatibility with the culture. Process consultants may play a key role in helping create the dispositions for discernment – helping articulate desires, tapping into generosity, facilitating the production of information from data-gathering and analysis, clarifying the role of hard thinking and prayerful reflection, and helping to deal with anxiety.

> *For process consultants to be maximally involved, they need to be skilled in facilitating prayerful decision-making.*

In process consultation, the guiding principle for the consultant is the collaborative working with the client in a manner that enables the client to develop his/her own diagnosis of the situation and the skills to act on it. The relationship is one where the client primarily defines the issues, sets the agenda and has control of the process and, therefore, can experience psychological success, develop skills, grow in trust of others and create effective group relations through this approach. This is contrasted with the approach where the consultant takes the most prominent role, defines the issues, maintains a professional distance through the power of expertise and, in essence, controls the situation. The attributes of the collaborative consultation approach are conceptually closely related to some counselling precepts. Carl Rogers, in describing the characteristics of a helping relationship, invites those in the helping role to face certain questions about their own dispositions. These dispositions relate to the ability to build trust, to allow oneself experience positive feelings towards the other, to be strong enough in oneself to allow freedom to the other, to be able to enter the world of the other and see things as he or she does, to be free from external evaluation, and to allow the other person to be in the process of becoming.

PHASES OF CONSULTATION

The consultation relationship between client and consultant typically has a number of phases. While these phases are described differently in many texts, there are some common strands. The initial phases are those where the client contacts the consultant, the relationship is explored and a formal and psychological contract is set. The psychological contract describes the form the consultation is to take, whether one based on consultant as expert or as process consultant. Then the setting and methods of work are agreed. For the process consultant, this may involve interviewing and observing and setting up processes whereby members of the organisation may address task and process issues which pertain to how the organisation functions. Each intervention creates its own opportunity for the consultant to help the client understand what is going on and so set up subsequent interventions. The process then is a cycle of intervention and review until the client is satisfied that the problem has been addressed or sufficient progress has been made. Then there is evaluation and disengagement by the consultant.

FACILITATION

The term *facilitation* refers to behaviours by individuals in group settings which help a group function. In its crudest it is a form of chairing a meeting, with some significant differences from traditional chairing methods and procedures. It has its origins in Carl Rogers' encounter groups. Rogers placed a great deal of emphasis on 'being a facilitative person' in a

Facilitation is about helping a group function.

group and saw that all group members could learn to perform that function, rather than it being the role of a designated person. In his view, as the members of a group learned to engage in facilitative behaviour, the 'facilitator' so-called could move to becoming a group member like the others.

Facilitation is about helping a group function. Because its origins lie in encounter groups, facilitation developed through a focus on the maintenance dynamics in group process. Facilitation meant attention to communication between group members, to how individuals were being heard and understood, how feelings were being received, and how individuals responded to others. In this way facilitation was a clear alternative to traditional chairing of meetings, which typically focuses on procedural rules as a means of agenda resolution. Facilitation was making a statement that people are important. Groups whose members wished to give particular attention to communication among its members frequently employed an outsider to facilitate the group. Hence the facilitator as a discrete role for hire came into being.

Over time, facilitation began to include task issues. Facilitative behaviour in a group not only focused on inter-personal communication but also on task clarification, role implementation, decision-making and problem-solving. Groups began to use facilitators to help them clarify their goals, set objectives and review progress. A more significant role for facilitators came into being – that of meeting designer. Facilitators now play a key role in designing meetings, that is setting up the structure and process by which a group will engage in its work. Designing meetings include: how to create a learning environment, macro-design issues such as outcomes, programme, structures, and micro issues such as length of sessions, timetabling and sequencing, managing the physical situation, such as seating, etc. For large group meetings, such as chapters and assemblies, these activities and skills are critical.

The art of facilitation involves a distinction between structuring and nondirectiveness. Structuring refers to what a facilitator does. In an assembly for example, there may be times when the whole assembly is in plenary session and other times when small groups meet. There may be ground-rules about sharing experience and forms of decision-making. Some elements of a meeting may be highly structured, others less so. There is no such thing as no structure. A lack of structure is in fact a structure.

Participants may feel they are being controlled or manipulated by a structure. This may be because the structure may stipulate what the discussion items are and so exclude other items. A critical question for facilitators, therefore, is the extent to which a designed structure enables or inhibits the clients to achieve their desired outcome. The skilled facilitator needs to be able to design structures which will enable the group members to achieve their desired outcomes, and also manage the process of these structures in a manner which is congruent with the values of self-determination.

Directive behaviour, in the broadest sense, guides, advises or coerces a client or group. Nondirective behaviour attempts to support, involve and enable the client or group in self-initiated and self-determined action. Directiveness-nondirectiveness is a continuum on which a facilitator chooses to implement structure. At the directive end of the continuum the facilitator imposes more structure or less structure on the group, while at the nondirective end the facilitator empowers the group in the process of self-determination.

Structuring and being nondirective are independent dimensions of facilitator behaviour. Structuring refers to what the facilitator does; directive-nondirective refers to *how* the facilitator does it. By a skilled use of both structuring and nondirectiveness, the facilitator hopes to release the energy of the group to achieve its own outcomes.

PROCESS CONSULTATION AND FACILITATION

Consultation and facilitation are not the same. Consultation may include facilitation. The consultant's role is more extensive than the facilitator's. A facilitator works in the

Consultation and facilitation are not the same.

context of a group meeting – whether a small or large group – and works to help that group achieve its desired outcomes. A consultant typically does a great deal of work outside of group meetings, individual meetings, observing people at work, and indeed may not actually facilitate any meetings. It is becoming more common that assemblies and chapters utilise both a consultant and facilitator. The facilitator performs the more public role of chairing sessions while the consultant may play a complementary role of observing and managing the process.

The following case example illustrates the distinction between consultant and facilitator. An individual who works as a consultant and facilitator was asked to facilitate a strategic planning meeting of a provincial and her council. When he met the group they sat around a table with a flip chart and they waited for him to begin. He asked some questions and wrote up the answers and so they proceeded. After about an hour he felt the atmosphere to be rather heavy and wondered whether they were making any progress. He shared his feeling and question with the group. It emerged that everyone felt they were not making any progress as the issues they were dealing with were not central to the current concerns of the provincial and her council. When they reflected on this together they saw that the facilitator was in an impossible position. He was facilitating a discussion of issues on which they were the experts. Because he did not know the complexities of the issues nor have the detailed background of the progress of these issues through their previous considerations, having him in the chairing-facilitating role was actually holding the discussion back.

Consequently, his role was renegotiated. He then became a process consultant to the group and one of the council took over the role of chairing the meeting. The council then began to discuss the issues as it needed to and he intervened with his questions as he saw fit. He sat and listened to the discussion and asked questions when he observed a lack of clarity, differing interpretations or uncertainty. He provided expert help on planning when required. The role change proved to be successful and the provincial and her council achieved their agenda to their satisfaction.

CONCLUSIONS

Using expert help from outside is an important aspect of any change process. This chapter has distinguished between different forms of professional help – from the expert who advises to the process consultant who helps clients resolve their own issues. A further distinction was made between consultation and facilitation. Facilitation involves the actual structuring and directing of group meetings. Religious as clients have to be clear about what sort of external help they want and need. They must learn what sort of consultant is required in a particular situation and how to use them. They must learn to know when to use a consultant rather than a facilitator, and be able to engage either or both in an appropriate contract.

CHAPTER 10

The Art of Leading
Apostolic Renewal

Leading change is an art, rather than a science or a cookbook of ready-to-make recipes. As for any artist, those leading change require some core theoretical frameworks from which to work, some tools to use and no small amount of skill. Underlying these theories, tools and skills is the general disposition of sensitivity to people, common sense and, of course, most important of all, a sense of God's grace. However, as this book has been focusing primarily on the organisational element of religious life and ministry, the emphasis in this final chapter remains on managing the complexities of a system, such as a province or an entire order.

Levels of Participation in Religious Life

One of the core constructs in understanding the dynamics of collective religious apostolic life is the framework of organisational levels. Organisational levels enable provincials to distinguish between the individual, the group/team/community, the co-ordination of multiple ministries across a province and the order ministering to God's people out of its charism and tradition. The levels framework focuses on how each level has its own task: vocational bonding for the individual, effective ministry for the ministry team, co-ordination for the province's ministries, and adaptation for the order in living out its charism in a changing world. The implications of distinguishing between levels are that provincials can use the framework as a tool for trying to understand what to do. Is a team or community having difficulty because the group is not agreed on its purpose or its way of working (Level II), or is it because an individual member has personal problems which are infecting the group (Level I)? Whatever the answer, any sort of remedial intervention must address the heart of the issue. Accordingly, each level must be approached differently. With respect to apostolic renewal, the renewal of individuals does not necessarily mean the renewal of the team or the aposto-late. If individuals have undergone a renewal, then further work needs to be done to help that individual renewal move to a team renewal. Similarly, a province renewal requires both individuals and teams/communities to have been renewed. In provinces, there are mechanisms for working at renewal at each of these levels. Individuals may attend courses and workshops; groups may organise renewal events for themselves – staff days, community/team meetings and so on. Provincial assemblies may mobilise the energy of a province around common issues. So it is not sufficient for provincials to work with individuals only (Level I); they must also understand and be able to work with groups (Level II) and with the relationships between groups (Level III).

A second issue with regard to the levels is that they are inter-dependent and inter-related. What happens at one affects each of the others. A provincial assembly may help individuals feel part of the province's direction and renew their bonding to the other mem-bers of the province. Individuals' commitment and openness may help the assembly be a success. An eye must always be kept to the effect of one level on another.

As the apostolic organisations in which religious participate are ventures in which religious and lay work side by side, the levels are not restricted to the narrow confines within religious life. For most religious, Level II dynamics involves working with lay colleagues in ministry teams. Level III dynamics are inclusive of ministries run by non-religious. Level IV takes in sharing charism with lay col-leagues and attempting to enable those who are not members of the order to find fulfilment and meaning their participation in the vision of their religious colleagues.

Strategic Thinking and Action

A second core construct is the area of strategy and its outcome in action. In its essence, strategy is about the relationship between fundamental purpose and conse-quent action. Strategic thinking is a mindset which addresses the big picture of what is significant in the light of identity and attempts to

> *In its essence, strategy is about the relationship between fundamental purpose and consequent action.*

form what is done. It is vividly contrasted with the details of day-to-day administration which are concerned with getting specific things done. Strategy is about direction, direction which is guided by identity and fundamental purpose. Its constituent elements are a clear sense of identity, a knowledge of the external world and of the limitations of available resources. Together, they are put together in a prayerful, discerning manner to form the basis for planning and action. There are several approaches to planning for action. It can be done formally in terms of creating a plan or incrementally in making the strategic decisions as they present themselves. Whatever the approach, each has its strengths and weaknesses.

Provincials as leaders play a key role in strategic thinking and action. They live in two time zones – the present, in administering their provinces, and the future, as architects of purpose. Whether they consciously address issues of the long-term future or not, provincials have a function in forming the future. Having no strategy is itself a strategy! Their own personal leadership behaviour plays an important role in creating the conditions whereby each of the levels functions to remain alive and engage in strategic thinking and action.

> *Having no strategy is itself a strategy!*

Leading Change

Provincials are not the generators of change. Frequently, they are the implementors of vision which comes from individuals and groups inside and outside their provinces. As implementors and architects of purpose, once they have accepted the need for change, they must take the change agenda to the four levels. That is, once a change agenda has been accepted, provincials take the role of actualising that agenda across the province, in individuals, ministry teams and communities and across ministries and communities. This involves two processes.

One process is the movement of the change agenda. This involves having a sense of the desired outcome, what needs to be done to get to that outcome, and the intermediary steps. What needs to be done, where, by whom and when. Underlying this is the ability to view the big picture before descending into detail. The second process follows from an understanding of how people change.

Whatever theory of change one might subscribe to, having an awareness of how people change is critical to developing a process which helps members feel safe, helps them participate and is sensitive to their perspective and feelings. Accordingly, processes aimed at helping commitment to change are equally important. Frequently, enrolling members of a province in task-forces, commissions and renewal groups is a mean of achieving both the furthering of the change agenda and involvement of the province.

Availing of external help is a significant element of any sort of change, whether personal or belonging to a larger system. The critical

How helpful is help?

question with regard to availing of help, whether through formal experts or informal channels is 'How is help helpful?' The different forms of help create different forms of psychological contract between helper and client. For provincials as clients, the critical issues are around what sort of help is useful and how it enables provincials to be strengthened in their roles as architects of purpose.

The challenges facing religious life into the new century are vibrant. There are new challenges to mission from increasing secularisation, the decline of the family, the need for religion and culture to dialogue, the ever-growing gap between the first and third worlds, those who can get jobs and those who cannot and so on. From within religious life there is the need to find new forms of religious life and ministry with decreasing numbers and a new sense of mission. All of these demand from religious orders an ability to adapt (Level IV) and be apostolic servants of Christ's mission in an ever-changing world. To be adaptive, religious orders need strategic leadership

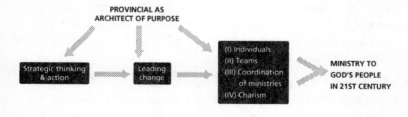

Figure 10-1
Leading renewal

and the skills to take collective action in the light of charism, vision, the analysis of needs and the resources available. Such action can be termed 'strategic' and undertaken in the spirit of the charism and a discerned sense of purpose.

This book has named some of the organisational themes inherent in the leadership of religious apostolic ministry into the future (Figure 10-1). Provincials, generals, directors of apostolates are architects of purpose. They stimulate the system to engage in strategic thinking and action and lead their provinces, orders and apostolates through a continuous process of change through an interaction of individuals, teams, groups and communities, and across teams, groups and communities to minister to God's people out of the charism of their foundation.

References and Further Reading

The books and articles referenced here are drawn largely from the organisation development literature and provide the sources for many of the ideas contained in this book. They are provided for those readers who wish to research the theory and practice of organisation development further.

CHAPTER 1:
LEVELS OF PARTICIPATION IN APOSTOLIC RELIGIOUS LIFE

Rashford, N.S., & Coghlan, D., *The Dynamics of Organizational Levels: A Change Framework for Managers and Consultants*, Addison-Wesley, Reading, MA., 1994

CHAPTER 2: PLANNING FOR STRATEGIC ACTION

Argyris, C., *Strategy, Change and Defensive Routines*, Pitman: Marshfield, MA., 1985.

Coghlan, D., 'The Apostolic Role of the Religious Bursar', *Religious Life Review*, November-December, 1989, 324-330.

Hax, A.C., & Majluf, *The Strategy Concept and Process*, Prentice-Hall: Englewood, Cliffs, NJ., 1991.

Mintzberg, H., 'Strategy Formation: Schools of Thought'. In J. Fredrickson, *Perspectives on Strategic Management*, Harper & Row: New York, 1990.

Mintzberg, H., Quinn, B.J., & James, R., *The Strategy Process*, Prentice-Hall: Englewood, Cliffs, NJ., 1989.

Monroe, T., 'Reclaiming Competence', *Review for Religious*, May-June 1992, 432-452.

Worley, C., Hitchin, D., & Ross, W., *Integrated Strategic Change*, Addison-Wesley: Reading, MA., 1996.

CHAPTER 3: STRATEGIC LEADERSHIP

Andrews, K., *The Concept of Corporate Strategy*, 2nd edition, Irwin: Homewood, Ill., 1990.

Beckhard, R., & Pritchard, W., *Changing the Essence: The Art of Creating and Leading Fundamental Change in Organizations*, Jossey-Bass: San Francisco, 1992.

Blake, R., & McCanse, A., *Leadership Dilemmas-Grid Solutions*, Gulf: Houston, 1991.

Nygren, D., & Ukeritis, M., 'Religious-Leadership Competencies', *Review for Religious*, 52, (May-June 1993), 390-417.

Schein, E.H., *Organizational Culture and Leadership*, 2nd edition, Jossey-Bass: San Francisco, 1992.

Wheatley, M., *Leadership and the New Science*, Berrett-Koehler: San Francisco, 1992.

PART 2: ORGANISATION DEVELOPMENT

Burke, W.W., *Organisation Development: a Process of Changing and Learning*, Addison-Wesley: Reading, MA., 1994.

Coghlan, D., 'Change Processes in Catholic Religious Orders'. In F. Massarik, (Ed.) *Advances in Organization Development*, Vol. 3, Ablex: Norwood, NJ., 1995.

French, W., & Bell, C., *Organization Development: Behavioural Science for Organizational Improvement*, 5th edition, Prentice-Hall: Englewood Cliffs, NJ., 1995.

Hanson P., & Lubin, B., *Answers to Questions Most Frequently Asked about Organization Development*, Sage: Thousand Oaks, CA., 1995.

Rothwell, W., Sullivan, R., & McLean, G., *Practicing Organisation Development*, Pfeiffer: San Diego, 1995.

Stacey, R., *Managing Chaos*, Kogan Page: London, 1992.

CHAPTER 4: UNDERSTANDING CHANGE

Bartunek, J.M. , 'Changing Interpretative Schemes and Organizational Restructuring: The Example of a Religious Order', *Administrative Science Quarterly*, Vol. 29, 1984, 355-372.

Bartunek, J.M., & Moch, M.K., 'Third-Order Organizational Change and the Western Mystical Tradition', *Journal of Organizational Change Management*, Vol. 7, 1994, No. 1, 24-41.

Coghlan, D., 'Change as Re-education: Lewin Revisited', *Organization Development Journal*, Vol. 12, 1994, No. 4, 1-7.

Coghlan, D., & Ottaway, R.N., 'Change Agents in Religious Life', *Human Development*, Vol. 11, 1990, No. 4, 38-42.

Lewin, K., 'Conduct, Knowledge and the Acceptance of New Values'. In K. Lewin, *Resolving Social Conflict: Selected Papers on Group Dynamics*, G. Lewin (Ed.) Souvenir Press, London, 1973.

Rashford, N.S., & Coghlan, D., *The Dynamics of Organizational Levels: A Change Framework for Managers and Consultants*, Addison-Wesley, Reading, MA., 1994.

Schein, E.H., *Organizational Psychology*, 3rd edition, Prentice-Hall, Englewood Cliffs, NJ., 1980.

Sperry, L., Passive Aggression in Organizations, *Human Development*, Vol. 11, 1990, No. 2, 40-45.

CHAPTER 5: MANAGING APOSTOLIC CHANGE

Beckhard, R., & Harris, R., *Organizational Transitions: Managing Complex Change*, 2nd edition, Addison-Wesley: Reading, Ma., 1987.

Rashford, N.S., & Coghlan, D., *The Dynamics of Organizational Levels: A Change Framework for Managers and Consultants*, Addison-Wesley: Reading, MA., 1994.

Worley, C., Hitchin, D., & Ross, W., *Integrated Strategic Change*, Addison-Wesley: Reading, MA., 1996.

CHAPTER 6: PHASES AND LEVELS OF APOSTOLIC RENEWAL

Bridges, W., *Managing Transitions*, Addison-Wesley, Reading, MA., 1991.

Rashford, N.S., & Coghlan, D., *The Dynamics of Organizational Levels: A Change Framework for Managers and Consultants*, Addison-Wesley, Reading, MA., 1994.

CHAPTER 7: GROUPS IN THE RENEWAL PROCESS

Beckhard, R., & Pritchard, W., *Changing the Essence: The Art of Creating and Leading Fundamental Change in Organizations*, Jossey-Bass: San Francisco, 1992.

Bushe, G.R., & Shani, A.B., *Parallel Learning Structures: Increasing Innovation in Bureaucracies*, Addison-Wesley: Reading, MA., 1991.

Rashford, N.S., & Coghlan, D., *The Dynamics of Organizational Levels: A Change Framework for Managers and Consultants*, Addison-Wesley: Reading, MA., 1994.

Reddy, W.B., & Jamison, K., *Team Building: Blueprints for Productivity and Satisfaction*, NTL-University Associates: Alexandria, VA-San Diego, CA., 1988.

Roemer, J., *The Group Meeting as a Contemplative Experience*, Jesuit Center for Spiritual Growth: Wernersville, PA., 1982.

Schein, E.H., 'How Can Organizations Learn Faster?', *Sloan Management Review*, Vol. 34, 1993, No. 2, 85-92.

CHAPTER 8: PROVINCIAL ASSEMBLIES

Coghlan, D., 'Towards Jerusalem – the Process of an Assembly', *Review for Religious*, Vol. 53, 1994, No. 6, 915-931.

Weisbord, M., and contributors, *Creating Common Ground*, Berrett-Koehler: San Francisco, 1992.

Weisbord, M., & Janov, S., *Future Search*, Berrett-Koehler: San Francisco, 1995.

CHAPTER 9: CONSULTATION AND FACILITATION

Coghlan, D., & McIlduff, E., 'Structuring and Nondirectiveness in Group Facilitation', *Person-Centered Review*, Vol. 5, 1990, No. 1, 13-29.

Heron, J., *The Facilitators' Handbook*, Kogan Page: London, 1989.

Nevis, E.C., *Organizational Consulting, A Gestalt Approach*, Gestalt Institute of Cleveland Press, 1988.

Reddy, W.B., *Intervention Skills*, Pfeiffer: San Diego, 1993.

Rogers, C.R., 'The Characteristics of a Helping Relationship', *The Carl Rogers Reader*, (Ed.) H Kirschenbaum & V.L. Henderson, Constable: London, 1990.

Schein, E.H., *Process Consultation, Vol. 1, Its Role in Organization Development*, 2nd edition, Addison-Wesley: Reading, MA., 1988.

Schein, E.H., *Process Consultation, Vol. 2, Lessons for Managers and Consultants*, Addison-Wesley: Reading, MA., 1987.

Schwarz, R.M., *The Skilled Facilitator*, Jossey-Bass: San Francisco, 1994.